Key Issues Number 29

LABOR-MANAGEMENT COMMITTEES: CONFRONTATION, COOPTATION, OR COOPERATION?

Charlotte Gold

ILR Press
New York State School of Industrial
and Labor Relations
Cornell University

ISSN: 0070-0185
ISBN: 0-87546-122-0

Library of Congress Number: 85-28489

Library of Congress Cataloging in Publication Data

Gold, Charlotte.
Labor-management committees.

(Key issues series, ISSN 0070-0185; no.29)
Bibliography: p.
Includes index.
1. Labor-management committees. 2. Management--Employee participation. I. Title. II. Series.
HD 6490.L33G64 1986 331'.01'12 85-28489
ISBN 0-87546-122-0

Copies may be ordered from
ILR Press
New York State School of Industrial and Labor Relations
Cornell University
Ithaca, New York 14851-0952
607/255-2264

CONTENTS

TABLES

INTRODUCTION

In the introduction to *Employer-Employee Committees and Worker Participation,* published in 1976, we noted that "Events in the 1970s—inflation, recession, diminishing levels of productivity, increased competition, and worker apathy—have caused a resurgence of interest in the United States in industrial cooperation..."(Gold 1976:1). That period began the flowering of a cooperative movement in the United States that saw a variety of joint labor-management projects appearing in both the private and public sectors. As a more recent study from the Conference Board, a private research firm, noted, "What was then considered experimental has become common practice in many companies" (Gorlin and Schein 1984:1). At this juncture, in the mid-1980s, it is useful to stop and look at what has transpired in the intervening years and evaluate the success of these programs.

In most evaluations of the prospects for labor-management cooperation in the United States ten years ago, the prognoses were relatively dim. While there was enthusiasm for the concept, the track record of such programs was not good. By any reckoning, there was little evidence of long-term institutionalization of cooperative projects within the economy. Thus, even the most enthusiastic proponents of cooperative efforts may well have had some doubts about their durability. Would the labor-management committees, quality of work life projects, and productivity sharing plans being instituted endure and be able to withstand the daily vicisitudes of industrial life or could they exist only in a carefully nurtured, hothouse environment? Would such programs play—and be perceived as playing—a central role in relations between employers and employees?

For that to happen, cooperative projects would have to achieve harmony with, and be embraced by, the unionized sector of the economy and would have to serve as the basis for a new working relationship in the nonunionized sector. Has that taken place?

Although it is too early to provide definitive answers to these questions, we can begin to make some preliminary evaluations. Thus, this report looks at where we have been, where we are now, and where we may be going. In doing so, our 1976 study (now out of print) is used throughout the report as a base for evaluating shifting trends over the decade. The title of the present work, *Labor-Management Committees: Confrontation, Cooptation, or Cooperation?,* reflects popular nomenclature on the subject, as well as a changing emphasis within the field.

In selecting the earlier title, *Employer-Employee Committees and Worker Participation,* we sought to convey the fact that the cooperative movement contained within it a wide variety of employer-employee committees. For the most part, however, the lay public and skilled professionals tend to think of all of them as labor-management committees, and we are doing the same here. In addition, while the question of the degree to which workers will participate in the decision-making process remains, it has not emerged as a central issue in this country. A subject that has continued to concern prospective participants is whether employees and unions may be coopted by engaging in the process. More recently, the fundamental question of whether it is even possible for American industry to move in a meaningful way from a posture of confrontation to one of cooperation has taken center stage. Thus, it is these topics—confrontation, cooptation, and cooperation—that are addressed here.

I

COOPERATIVE PROGRAMS: TYPES AND GOALS

In any discussion of labor-management committees, the key word is *cooperation*: working together, rather than in an adversarial relationship, toward a common end or purpose. In the early 1970s, when the notion of cooperation between labor and management was viewed as a solution to the ill effects of "foreign penetration of domestic markets, inadequate capital investment, inflation, U.S. businesses fleeing to the third world, slow productivity growth, high interest rates" (Stepina 1982:1), and a host of other problems, there was uncertainty as to just how cooperation would now work in this country. How would it differ from programs in the past or from the European experience, with the evolving trend there toward worker participation in management? What role would it play in the unionized and nonunionized sectors? What types of projects would prove to be the most durable? The past ten years have provided us with some answers to these questions and we now have the benefit of talking about what has been as opposed to what might be.

Despite the fact that joint committees have long been considered the exception rather than the rule in the United States, they have been used with varying degrees of success for more than sixty years and have operated at the national, industry, regional, community, plant, and production-unit levels. Traditionally in the past, they existed in unionized firms where "labor" is considered synonymous with "union" and where collective bargaining is the major mode of interaction between management and its employees. Labor-management committees in this setting serve as a supplement to collective bargaining.

During the more recent resurgence of interest in employer-employee cooperation over the past ten years, however, programs have been implemented in both unionized and nonunionized firms. Although precise figures are not available, it is generally agreed that labor-management committees of all kinds were more common in the 1970s than in the 1960s (Anderson and Feuille 1981:2) and their numbers have encreased even more during the last decade. In 1982, John Hoerr (1982:26) of *Business Week* noted that the quality of work life (QWL) programs—just one type of cooperative program implemented in both unionized and nonunionized firms—were known to be under way in at least seven hundred plants, even though they were relatively rare ten years before. In the latter part of 1984, it was estimated that more than two million workers were active participants in employee involvement programs. That same year, 41 percent of the companies with more than five hundred employees surveyed by the New York Stock Exchange indicated that they had worker-management participation programs (Serrin 1984:128, 136).

The presence of cooperative committees brings up questions concerning their legality that have been raised since the mid-1930s. In recent years, the issue of participation programs in unionized firms, where such programs exist but are not controlled by unions, has been addressed by Donna Sockell (1984), who refers to the "dubious legality of employee-participation mechanisms" under such circumstances. She notes that although the National Labor Relations Board (NLRB) to date has not heard any cases resulting from objections to these programs, she believes that the NLRB and the courts "would rule that the committee is violating the union's exclusivity; and the employer in dealing with that committee, is violating §8(a) (5) of the NLRA," the section that prohibits an employer from circumventing the collective bargaining agent or abrogating its duty to bargain collectively. Sockell, however, also points out that despite strong reservations expressed by some union leaders about employee-participation structures not under union control, these programs appear to be thriving, with the union leadership adopting a "wait and see" attitude (1984:554, 542).

At the same time, other unions actively support new efforts to achieve labor-management cooperation. In 1982, citing just one example, local representatives of the International Association of Machinists and Aerospace Workers (IAM) were involved in eighty-eight labor-management committees and twenty-six quality circles, although only 30 percent of the former and 77 percent of the latter were provided for by collective agreement (Birbaum 1982:51).

In what follows, we will consider the overall goals of cooperative programs, as well as the distinct types of projects that are currently functioning in American firms.

Goals

Some proponents of joint committees are interested primarily in greater productivity, but see employee satisfaction as an added benefit. Others consider increased employee satisfaction, achieved through improving the quality of work life, to be the main purpose of these efforts, with increased efficiency and improvement in the quality of goods produced as fortuitous side effects. In each case, however, greater economies and increased worker satisfaction are the goals, although given different weight depending on the perspective. Advocates of cooperation therefore support committee programs and other activities for a combination of economic and social reasons, as well as on ethical and political grounds.

Perhaps the most interesting development over the past decade has been the increased willingness on the part of U.S. companies to experiment with and implement alternative management styles that encourage a degree of direct employee participation in decisions governing the work process. Managers in firms are being encouraged to delegate responsibility and, in some instances, act more as consultants, resource people, and planners. At the same time, trade unionists are being asked to modify their traditional views of labor-management relations and some have become involved in joint programs where the emphasis is on problem solving rather than on confrontation.

A basic characteristic of the majority of cooperative programs is that they are composed of workers and representatives of management who come together to discuss problems at the workplace that are assumed to be of common interest to them. Employees become involved in activities of the enterprise beyond their principal job responsibilities. Thus, even if workers talk only about managerial decisions affecting their own work, this constitutes an extension of their normal job duties. The purpose of these programs is to take advantage of an employee's capabilities, involve workers in decisions affecting their jobs, and provide employees with greater identification with organizational goals in an effort to improve the overall efficiency of the firm. Some supporters of employee involvement believe that in the course of sharing in managerial decision making, workers find solutions to problems "that no outside manager could possibly imagine" (Serrin 1984:128).

Varieties of Programs

Cooperative programs can be divided into three broad categories: those that are implemented within an organization (on a companywide or inplant basis), those functioning within an industry, and those covering a variety of establishments within an area or region. During the past decade, there has been growing experimentation by various groups with a variety of programs: labor-management committees, productivity sharing plans, and quality of work life projects. The following brief history of these programs is from Gold (1976:15-18), based primarily on Derber (1970a) and Slichter (1941).

Labor-Management Committees: A Brief History

While there had been sporadic experimentation with different forms of worker representation plans in the United States in the late 1800s and the first part of the 1900s, it was not until the National War Labor Board encouraged the widespread development of shop committees and work councils to improve productivity during World War I that the number began to increase. At its 1918 convention, the American Federation of Labor (AFL) also urged its members to work cooperatively in committees with management to deal with matters of production.

The National War Labor Board pressed for representation plans in nonunion enterprises with the thought that these plans would lead to unionization. Although many plans were terminated by employers at the end of World War I, over a million workers in such companies as General Electric, Bethlehem Steel, and Goodyear Tire and Rubber Company were still participants in 1924.

Employee representation plans became a critical issue for unions that were seeking recognition at this time. Employee representation in nonunion firms was viewed by some labor relations specialists as an honest democratic alternative to collective bargaining but by others as a mechanism to deter unionization. The former assumed that mutual economic interest could not exist between employees and employers in a collective bargaining setting and that employees should not equate an increase in bargaining power with a rise in benefits. The latter considered employees involved in cooperative schemes as members of company unions and tools of management.

In a comparison of nonunion shop committees and trade unions conducted in 1920 (at which time approximately 19 percent of the nonfarm work force were union members), Paul Douglas found that the nonunion shop committees were generally employer-dominated and limited in function to the consideration of unimportant matters. Committee decisions were often subject to executive approval, committee membership restricted by a number of qualifications, and employee members reluctant to take a stand because of possible reprisals. Douglas did see hope, however, for shop committees that functioned side by side with negotiating committees in unionized firms.

Union membership had grown rapidly during World War I, but in the early 1920s unions met with increased management resistance. Confronted with a depression in 1921, the unions in the textile and railroad industries became more interested in cooperation as a way to establish better relations with management, while increasing output, reducing costs, and ensuring their members employment in the face of nonunion competition.

As did the National War Labor Board in World War I, the War Production Board began a drive in 1942 to encourage the establishment of joint labor-management production committees. Labor-management cooperation was sought to produce sufficient goods to meet wartime needs, reduce conflict, control inflation, and ensure adequate manpower. The committees met to consult on absenteeism, health and safety, training, and general personnel issues in order to achieve greater efficiency. Some of these committees developed extensive programs; others sponsored only a single event. There were approximately five thousand such committees in plants employing almost seven million workers operating at one time or another during the war.

Dorothea de Schweinitz (1949), in one of the most comprehensive studies of labor-management cooperation in this period, reported that only a few hundred committees contributed significantly to improving productivity. She did find additional benefits, however, in the more successful cases. Among other things, she found that union-management cooperation was extended to industries that had never experienced it before. It also became more apparent that workers had ideas to contribute to the running of the enterprise and that there could be increased output and improved quality in organizations that were already fairly efficient. Another critic of these programs, Clinton Golden, a regional director of the Steelworkers, writing in the journal *The Annals*, claimed, on the other hand, that labor-management committees were sometimes substituted for regular grievance committees and that the programs lacked central planning, provided no protection for workers displaced by the introduction of new technology, and did not provide for the equitable distribution of the proceeds of increased productivity (in Derber 1970a:380-81).

Few U.S. labor-management committees continued after the war. In an unpublished report on joint productivity committees prepared by the Bureau of Labor Statistics (BLS) in 1974, the BLS described six cases in which joint committees were mandated in labor contracts. A 1963-64 BLS study had found forty-four contracts calling for joint committees; in 1972, this number had dropped to twenty-two. Of these twenty-two, fourteen provided for discussion of mutual problems, but gave no authority to the committees to seek solutions, and three had been negotiated by a government agency, the TVA (Raskin 1975:1).

Recent Developments in Inplant and Industrywide Labor-Management Committees

A brief overview of labor-management committees in the 1980s reveals how extensively they have proliferated. In 1984, for example, the Ford Motor Company had eighty-six worker participation programs operating in fifteen states and each of General Motors 151 American facilities had some form of participation program, ranging from those operating in sections involving fifty to two hundred workers to more extensive activities (Serrin 1984:136).

In March 1980, the Xerox Corporation and the Amalgamated Clothing and Textile Workers Union (ACTWU) agreed to establish problem-solving teams in the company's four manufacturing plants. A year later, there were over ninety such teams, and in 1983, Xerox and the ACTWU signed a new contract committing both parties to joint programs and expanding them into other noncompetitive areas (Lazes and Costanza 1984:1, 7).

Since 1982, staff members at the New York State School of Industrial and Labor Relations at Cornell University have been engaged in Programs for Employment and Workplace Systems (PEWS), working with management, labor, and community leaders to develop cooperative strategies in their organizations so that they could remain competitive, save jobs, and increase employment. A list of organizations that have received technical assistance and training or have been involved in workshops or conferences includes the ACTWU and Xerox, Bell Laboratories, the Beaumont Shipyard, Bethlehem Steel Corporation, Hyatt-Clark Industries, the International Association of Machinists and Aerospace Workers, and the Sun Shipbuilding and Drydock Company (PEWS brochure, n.d.).

In railroading, the Milwaukee Road has engaged in a joint program with seventeen labor organizations representing craft employees. Through their Labor Management Action Group, the parties have worked on changing operating practices and work rules, improving disciplinary procedures, and effectuating materials reclamation. A similar program has functioned with the Houston Belt and Terminal Railway and the United Transportation Union and the Brotherhood of Railway, Airline and Steamship Clerks, Freight Handlers, Express and Station Employes.

On an industrywide basis, labor-management committees are operating in both the private and public sectors. Selected examples include a labor-management program covering ten thousand carpenters in Oregon functioning through the Oregon State District Council of Carpenters. In Indiana, the Fraternal Order of Police and the Professional Fire Fighters Union, together with the Indiana Association of Cities and Towns, work through Indiana University in a cooperative effort. The state of Delaware has established a labor-management committee for its employees. The Clackamas County [Oregon] Labor-Management Committee includes among its projects a joint health care cost containment program for county employees.

Although, as previously noted, labor-management committees may be established in unionized firms without union participation, often they are set up through the joint efforts of labor and management. Under these circumstances, they require a degree of cooperation between the two major participants even before they are formed. In the past, those pessimistic about such committees have pointed to the essential adversarial relationship that exists between unions and management, which tends to undermine cooperative efforts. But, as many students of collective bargaining in the United States have pointed out, to characterize that relationship as totally adversarial is not accurate. Unions and employers could not function together if a certain amount of cooperation was not achieved and maintained. Labor-management committees are grounded in that cooperative spirit and seek to enlarge and expand upon it. While cooperation may not come easily in some settings, especially where relations have been strained in the past, economic problems in the 1970s and 1980s have caused both groups to see the greater need for collaboration, rather than confrontation.

Inherent in the process is the agreement to try to improve the industrial relations climate. One of the initial goals of such committees is to produce a change in attitude between union leadership and management and between management and employees. As Michael Schuster (1983:193) points out, "The focus is on problem-solving activities and building trust."

Experience has shown that labor and management groups that wish to establish new cooperative ventures within the enterprise must first determine where their collective bargaining relationship ends and the work of their new cooperative committees will begin. In a real sense, many such committees in unionized firms stem from the collective bargaining relationship, with their charters serving as addenda to the collective bargaining agreement or as separate letters of understanding. An example of one such agreement—between the Ford Motor Company and the United Automobile Workers of America (UAW)—is as follows:

Excerpt from Letter of Understanding—Ford Motor Company and the UAW, 1979

During 1979 negotiations, Ford Motor Company and the UAW discussed at length the potential benefits of increased involvement of employees in matters affecting their work. Employee involvement, we agreed, holds promise for aiding and expanding efforts of the Company and the Union to make work a more satisfying and stimulating experience.

Constructive efforts to involve employees to a degree in relevant workplace matters may also enhance employee creativity, contribute to improvements in the workplace, support goals of achieving the highest quality products, heighten efficiency, and reduce unwarranted absenteeism.

The parties agreed to provide joint management and union leadership and support to increased levels of employee involvement. Accordingly, a National Joint Committee on Employee Involvement is established, composed of three (3) members appointed by the Vice President, Director of the UAW National Ford Department, and three (3) members appointed by the Vice President-Labor Relations, Ford Motor Company.... The National Joint Committee will...have responsibility for:

(a) Reviewing and evaluating existing programs which involve improving the work environment of Ford employees represented by the UAW.

(b) Developing new concepts and pilot projects including:

__Actions which encourage voluntary employee partricipation in identifying and solving work-related problems. Autonomous work groups, team building and quality circles are examples of matters for joint consideration.

__Actions directed at minimizing the disruptive effects of unwarranted absenteeism on employees and on operations....

__Examination of alternative work schedules designed to improve the work climate, to increase the utilization of facilities, and to reduce absenteeism and its effects (from Gorlin and Schein 1984:12).

When committees were first formed in this country, it was largely assumed that the cooperative process should be kept separate from the negotiations process and the grievance procedure. This distinction between bargaining and nonbargaining issues is zealously maintained in some organizations today. According to an agreement between U.S. Steel and the United Steelworkers of America (USW), for example, grievance procedures and terms of the basic labor agreement are excluded from the jurisdiction of the participation teams. Instead, the parties consider product quality, safety and environmental health, scheduling arrangements, absenteeism, overtime, bonus payments, changes in incentive-performance pay, job alignment, and transportation pools. (The USW has also established joint committees with Bethlehem Steel Corporation, Jones & Laughlin Steel Corporation, Republic Steel, and National Steel Corporation. These programs are discussed more fully in chapter three.)

Problem-solving teams at the Xerox Corporation are not permitted to investigate either economic or business problems or to "tamper with the collective bargaining agreement." Permissible subjects of investigation are product quality; work environment safety; savings in material and inventory costs; improvements in process, methods, or systems and in facilities, tools, or equipment; reduction in paperwork; elimination of waste materials and supplies; quality; scrap; rework; and the location of equipment and materials. Nonpermissible subjects are salaries, union grievances, the union contract, benefits, company policy, working hours, rates, breaks, classifications, overtime, personalities, the payroll, discipline, problems on which shop chairmen are working, and production standards (Lazes and Costanza 1984:2).

In other organizations, however, participants have felt that in divorcing the work of the cooperative committees from what takes place in collective bargaining and the grievance procedure, the committees were left with what they considered to be minor issues. This feeling is apparent in the view expressed by two researchers in 1970 when they said, "in the free world, at least, unsuccessful councils handle trivia; successful ones bargain" (Strauss and Rosenstein 1970:206). What has happened as a consequence is that in these organizations, certain proscribed subjects handled solely through negotiations in the past have gradually come to be discussed in joint committees as well. Changes growing out of these committees may result in modifications of or additions to the collective bargaining agreement, either when negotiations are reopened or as attached memos of understanding to the existing contract.

Glenn Watts, president of the Communications Workers of America (CWA), agrees that certain aspects of cooperative programs are viewed by many in the labor movement as a threat. "But others—and I include myself among them—see it as offering a great opportunity to extend the reach of collective bargaining." He adds that the collective bargaining process has not been weakened. "We work on the traditional issues of wages and basic working conditions just as we always have. But through QWL, we are extending our influence into the murky territory of 'management prerogatives,' helping to shape management practices and policies while they are being formed rather than after the fact" (Watts 1983:13).

In general, though, labor-management committees handle such issues as improving employee morale, solving production and workplace problems, stabilizing employment, and developing training and retraining programs. Table 1 is a brief summary of opportunities created by such committees.

Table 1

Summary of Opportunities Created by Cooperative Union-Management Programs

Performance Indicators	Employee Outcomes	Relationship Changes
Productivity improvement	Increase job satisfaction	Attitude change among key actors
Reduce labor costs	Job influence and involvement	Union influence on key decisions
Quality improvements	Information about job and company	Reduce likelihood of future strikes
Product design changes	Commitment to company	Reduce grievances
Reduce absenteeism	Improve conditions of work	Better understanding of L-M issues
Reduce turnover	Improve supervision	Examine outdated contract language
Reduce tardiness	Reduce job frustration	Continuous study of on-going problems
Reduce accidents	Improve earnings	Facilitate technological change
Improve manpower utilization	Upgrade job characteristics	
	Increase trust	
	Increase job security	

Source: Schuster 1983:192. Reprinted with permission of the Industrial Relations Research Association ©1983.

The experience of the San Francisco General Hospital and its employees bears out the notion that participating parties in a labor-management committee often need a formal structure and "contract" in which rules and responsibilities are spelled out. In 1980, a committee was established in the Medical Records Division of the Radiology Department with hospital personnel and Service Employees' International Union (SEIU) Local 400 Medical Records workers. An early verbal agreement guaranteed committee members 10 percent of any savings on revenues generated through extraordinary efforts that were not within the "normal scope of job-related duties." The committee redesigned and reorganized billing procedures that resulted in $350,000 in increased revenues for the hospital. While committee members saw this as an innovation apart from their day-to-day activities, top management did not and the members "abruptly abandoned their efforts to work cooperatively, with much anger, confusion, and lingering hostility over this experience" (Schraeger 1983:13).

The same year, however, the San Francisco Labor-Management Work Improvement Project, a longer lasting and more successful project, was established as the formal vehicle for city unions, members of management, and employees to address issues of mutual concern. The city has approximately 27,000 public employees, represented by some twenty-five public employee unions. Labor-management committees have been established in the Housing Authority, the Department of Public Works, the Department of Recreation and Parks, and the Public Utilities Commission. Barbara Schraeger, the project director, finds that these committees are providing a much needed vehicle for cooperation. She concludes that the existing labor-management committees have had a positive effect on attitudes in other departments:

> Many City departments and City employee unions who are not involved in labor-management committees have expressed interest in learning about a cooperative process that serves the needs of all participants. While some employees are resistant to change efforts, it appears that there is a genuine willingness on the part of most City managers and employee unions to take a new approach to operating the City. They are ready to move away from their traditional adversarial positions and align themselves toward the common goal of work improvement. The challenge lies in helping those who are ready for change to unravel old patterns and attitudes and to encourage those who are not to grow toward change (Schraeger 1983:15).

Area Labor-Management Committees

In 1976 we reported on what we described as a "novel plan for a community-level committee" operating in Jamestown, New York, since 1972. What was once novel has now become more commonplace in various areas and regions thoughout the United States.

In addition to the Jamestown program, there are a number of cooperative efforts under way throughout the country, but they are particularly prevalent in the Northeast and Midwest,* regions in which "unemployment is high; companies and

---

* Programs include the Michigan Quality of Work Life Council, the Siouxland [Iowa] Labor-Management Committee, the Northeast Labor-Management Center [Boston-based], the Chemung County [New York] Labor-Management Committee, the Philadelphia Area Labor-Management Committee, the Chautauqua County [New York] Labor-Management Committee, the Kankakee County [Illinois] Labor-Management Committee, the Kenosha [Wisconsin] Labor-Management Council, Inc., the Economic Development Council of Northeastern Pennsylvania, the Duluth Area Labor-Management Association, Inc., the Lansing [Michigan] Area Joint Labor-Management Committee, Inc., the Cumberland [Maryland] Area Labor-Management Committee, and a committee in Clinton, Pennsylvania.

unions are perceived as having poor labor-management relations; the population and, hence, the labor force are declining, there is a high degree of unionization; and the local economic base is deteriorating" (Leone 1983:174). The program established in Jamestown, a city of 75,000 in the southwestern tip of New York State, sixty-five miles from Buffalo, continues to be representative of the type of program set up in these two sections of the country. The following description of the early years of the Jamestown program is from Gold (1976:31-33).

In the early 1970s, Jamestown was a deteriorating industrial community. It had an increasing unemployment rate (near 10 percent in 1971, when the rate for the state ranged between 5.5 and 6.1 percent that year), a decreasing number of manufacturing jobs, and a history of poor labor relations. The full impact of this situation was brought home to local residents when Art Metal Corporation, one of the area's largest manufacturers, closed its new one-million-square-foot plant and left seven hundred workers unemployed.

Through the combined efforts of the city's mayor, its ombudsman, a representative of the Manufacturers' Association of the Jamestown Area, a mediator from the Buffalo office of the Federal Mediation and Conciliation Service, a leader of a major union in the area, and an attorney, a communitywide labor-management committee was formed in 1972. Its purpose was to improve labor relations, encourage manpower development, provide assistance to industrial development programs, and work toward gains in productivity.

During January 1972, separate meetings were held with executives of fifteen local manufacturing companies and union officials representing employees in these plants. In February, a joint session was convened. From that meeting came the decision to organize an ongoing committee composed of approximately thirty-six members, with equal representation from labor and management. Later this committee was expanded to include fifty members. The function of the committee was to (a) establish and guide smaller committees in local plants, (b) hold meetings, seminars, and conferences on related topics, (c) encourage skills development programs, and (d) provide leadership. The committee became known as the Jamestown Area Labor-Management Committee (JALMC).

The actual administrative business of the committee was carried on by a ten-member executive board. The board was composed of four manufacturing executives and four labor representatives, together with the executive vice president of the Manufacturers' Association of the Jamestown Area and a member of the AFL-CIO Central Labor Council. This board was jointly chaired by a representative from labor and one from management, and from time to time, it established small task forces to undertake special studies and initiate new projects.

In 1973 a full-time coordinator was hired. His job was to investigate local conditions, coordinate existing programs, and serve as a convener and resource person for inplant committees. He helped these committees to get started and took on a quasi-mediation role. He also located individuals to provide training in response to particular needs. The coordinator reported to and received instructions from the executive board.

Approximately eighteen companies and eleven unions were soon affiliated with the labor-management committee. The companies were primarily manufacturing firms operating in the areas of fabricated metals, engineering products, glass and ceramics, and wood furniture. They ranged from large companies owned by international conglomerates to small local businesses. They produced such goods as sheet metal, ball bearings, furniture, radiators, and washing machines. The unions included, among others, the International Association of Machinists and Aerospace Workers, the United Furniture Workers of America, and the United Steelworkers.

By 1974, two years after the area labor-management committee in Jamestown was started, the unemployment rate had dropped well below the state average and the area was relatively strike-free. During the two years, there were five minor strikes with a loss of 41 working days as compared to eight strikes and 302 lost days in the preceding three years. Between 1969 and 1971, there was a net loss of 2,100 manufacturing jobs in the county; between 1972 and 1974 there was a net gain of 1,100.

During this period, Jamestown attracted a major new business, Cummins Engine Company, to fill the $10.5-million plant left empty by the closing of the Art Metal Corporation. On the negative side, a large company, Crescent Tool and Machine, made the decision to move to South Carolina.

By 1985, the JALMC had expanded into the public sector, with on-going public sector joint committees at the Jamestown Community College, City Hospital, and City School System. At the same time, the JALMC continues to be active in the private sector.

Martin D. Hanlon and John C. Williams (1982) find that the overall success rate of area committees in improving productivity and the quality of work life is higher in Jamestown than in the country as a whole. Among the committee's general accomplishments, they cite its ability to remain in operation continuously despite drops in funding and changes in personnel. (In 1982 the municipal government was the major source of operating funds.) They point out that the committee has continued to help slow the exodus of manufacturing jobs from Jamestown. Between 1972 and 1981, 824 jobs were saved, according to JALMC calculations, and 1,413 jobs were added. Days lost due to work stoppages declined dramatically and although hard data are scarce, many believe that grievances declined due to the committee's efforts. In addition, Hanlon and Williams find that informal communication among firms allows for more extensive innovation (1982:4-8).

Quality of Work Life Programs

A list of U.S. companies engaged in some form of quality of work life (QWL) program (often combined with productivity improvement efforts) is impressive.*

Under QWL, which generally refers to efforts to improve the work environment for the individual by providing opportunities for personal accomplishment and participation in organizational decisions, are such activities as job redesign and problem solving. Problem-solving groups are known by many names—quality circles, quality teams, worker circles, employee-participation groups, or employee-involvement teams. But, for the most part, all are shop-level worker committees that attempt to use statistical and problem-solving analysis to improve quality and productivity in a work area.

QWL programs tend to be used more frequently in nonunion companies, but there are a number of notable examples of QWL programs in unionized settings. General Motors and the United Auto Workers began a joint program in 1973, which continues in effect today. In 1980, the American Telephone and Telegraph Company (AT&T) and the Communications Workers of America (CWA) implemented a similar program based on a memorandum of agreement covering half a million workers in twenty-one Bell system companies.

In the public sector, New York State and the Civil Service Employees Association (CSEA), representing over 100,000 state workers in three bargaining units, agreed, in the course of negotiating their 1979-1982 contracts, to engage in a joint QWL program. The objectives of the program are to improve productivity and the work life of employees and to further labor-management relations. (Since 1972, CSEA, the state, and several other unions with which it deals had been engaged in a variety of joint labor-management activities.) A statewide Committee on the Work Environment and Productivity, composed of twenty-one members and organized into three subcommittees, considers implementing programs to deal with such matters as hours of work, physical working conditions, job tasks, job stress and strain, control and influence over work, social support and relationships, career development and advancement, and relationships between work and an employee's

---

* A brief sample includes Westinghouse Electric Corporation; Inland Steel; Xerox; American Telephone and Telegraph; Hewlett-Packard; Northrop Corporation's Aviation Division; Baxter Travenol Laboratories, Inc.; Eaton Corporation; Dana Corporation; Honeywell, Inc.; The Pillsbury Company; Shaklee Corporation; Kaiser Aluminum and Chemical Corporation; General Motors; Security Pacific National Bank; Manufacturers Hanover Trust Company; Fireman's Fund Insurance Companies; Citibank, N.A.; Prudential Insurance Company of America; Metropolitan Life Insurance Company; Lear Siegler, Inc.; Sun Chemical Corporation; Ebasco Services, Inc.; Harley-Davidson Motor Company; Atlantic Richfield Company; International Business Machines; Minnesota Mining and Manufacturing Company; and Hughes Aircraft Company.

personal and family life. The subcommittees, however, do not concern themselves with questions of wages and job security. In the productivity area, they address such issues as individual and group work output, absenteeism and tardiness, turnover, interpersonal conflict, and personal problems (CWEP/QWL&P 1981).

In 1986, James B. Northrup, director of the Workforce Planning Unit, reported that collaborative labor-management activities were still very much in evidence in New York State. One example is the proliferation of employee assistance programs jointly funded by the state and all of the unions with which it bargains. These programs are designed to aid employees with alcohol and drug problems, as well as to assist them with other financial and personal matters. Work sharing/job sharing and day care services for children of state employees continue to be a focus of mutual concern. In conjunction with two unions, the CSEA and the Professional Employees Federation, the state is exploring the issue of increased employment security. Recent rounds of bargaining produced funding for joint committees that will investigate the possibility of eliminating layoffs for a reduced workforce (phone conversation with author, January 15, 1986).

Michael Maccoby, a consultant to AT&T and CWA, has noted that in a unionized setting, QWL programs often grow out of the collective bargaining process. "It is a commitment of management and union to support localized activities and experiments to increase employee participation in determining how to improve work. This process is guided by union-management committees and facilitators, and requires education about the goals of work and training in group process" (Maccoby 1984:29).

The Conference Board, in a 1984 study covering 153 companies (of which 80 percent were engaged in manufacturing), found that different varieties of cooperative programs "rarely exist in isolation from each other. Combinations...are found in the same company, in the same plant, and often in the same workplace." The study goes on to cite the presence of such combinations as productivity sharing programs, problem-solving groups, and job redesign in a single company. TRW, for example, has constructed several new plants, which were built with an eye toward establishing innovative management systems. Known as "greenfield plants," they are participatively managed facilities with a minimum of formal supervisors and a major reliance on autonomous or self-managed work teams. (Greenfield plants are, for the most part, nonunion.) In a unionized facility, TRW has instituted a productivity sharing plan (Scanlon). Quality circles are in operation at forty-five locations and the company has also instituted a special management development program to deal with managerial behavior, team building, conflict resolution, strategic planning, and feedback (Gorlin and Schein 1984:17).

Productivity Sharing Plans

Productivity sharing plans generally combine worker participation in decision making with a group incentive plan that rewards workers for productivity gains. In general, three different types of profit sharing plans have been put into effect in American companies:

> Cash (Current): where profit shares are paid out directly (immediately) in cash (or stock) to employees.
>
> Deferred: where profit shares are paid into a trust fund on behalf of individual employees, separate participant accounts are created, the monies are invested (e.g., in own company stock, stock of other companies, bonds, real estate) and distributed to participants at a later contingency—i.e., at retirement, death, disability, severance, or during employment (under partial or total withdrawal provisions).
>
> Combination: where part of the profit share is paid out directly in cash and part is deferred into a trust fund (Metzger 1974:19).

The best known is the Scanlon Plan, which involves an employee suggestion program, committee system, and bonus formula based on the relationship between sales value of production and labor costs. A related program, the Rucker Plan, also has a suggestion program and a bonus formula, but provides for a more limited committee system. This plan is based on the historic relationship in American industry between the "value added" (the difference between the costs of materials and supplies that go into a product and its sales price) and payroll costs. The objective of the plan is to increase value added by achieving greater cost savings. A related plan, Improshare (IMproved PROductivity through SHARing), has little or no employee participation. A bonus formula is based on engineering standards and hours worked. A relatively new program, Improshare seeks to increase output for fewer hours of input. Productivity gain is expressed as the number of hours saved for a specified number of units produced compared to a prior base period.

When the Scanlon Plan came into prominence in the United States following World War II, it was a unique experiment in employee participation and gain sharing. The following brief discussion of this approach to labor-management cooperation is from Gold (1976:25) and Gorlin and Schein (1984:10-11).

Joseph Scanlon, an accountant, steelworker, labor official, and later a faculty member at the Massachusetts Institute of Technology, developed the plan in the late 1930s. It achieved national recognition with its introduction into the LaPointe Machine Tool Company in 1947. The plan relied on a suggestion system and a set of departmental committees designed to involve all workers actively in the functioning of the organization. It called for workers understanding why they undertook certain tasks; consensus between management, unions, and workers on common goals; an opportunity for input by everyone involved; and full information on matters relating to the operation of the enterprise. Joint production committees, in which workers and managers developed suggestions to reduce labor costs, played an essential part in this approach to labor-management cooperation.

The plan uses historical experience in a plant to establish labor costs as a percentage of sales dollars. A base ratio is determined by dividing payroll by sales, plus or minus inventory. A bonus is granted when labor costs are less than the base ratio in any given month. When cost savings are effected, a small part is usually set aside for capital expenditures and the rest is distributed to employees on a monthly basis.

Scanlon Plans have been used in both union and nonunion facilities. In unionized plants, the plan is nonnegotiable and does not become an issue in bargaining. In both types of plants, the terms of the plan are developed by a joint labor-management committee and the plan is adopted by vote of the employees. The Conference Board concludes that the plan tends to be successful in smaller facilities, that is, plants with under five hundred employees.

The Board cites the example of one such program in the Dana Corporation. Production committees typically consist of a foreman, tool engineer, and two to four elected departmental representatives. They meet monthly to solicit suggestions, review recommendations, and implement low-cost suggestions. Production committees report to the plant steering committee, which is composed of the plant manager and representatives of the production committees and managerial staff. The steering committee considers monthly productivity performance, calculates the bonus, and reviews more costly suggestions. The plan at Dana requires interest by 80 percent of the plant membership and is renewable from year to year.

II

AMERICAN VIEWS ON PARTICIPATION

An essential issue at the heart of all cooperative efforts is the level of real participation that exists and the degree of decision-making authority that is delegated to employees. The U.S. experience in this respect differs markedly from that of some work organizations in Western Europe. At the same time, firms within the United States also vary in the participative potential built into the change technique—that is, in the extent to which workers can be involved in decision making.

Limits to Participation

In considering the difference between America and Europe, "it is necessary to distinguish between those schemes which seek to give full control of industry as a matter of principle and those which introduce a measure of involvement as a solution to practical difficulties. The former should be termed industrial democracy or worker control, the latter worker participation" (Robbins 1972:430).

Expanding on this distinction, George Strauss and Eliezer Rosenstein (1970:202-3) suggest that we are dealing with two approaches: socialist (industrial democracy) and human relations (worker participation). The socialist approach is involved more with the structural formalities of ownership and representation, while the human relations approach deemphasizes formal power structures. The human relations approach holds that, while the decision-making process should be humanized, the principle of management prerogatives is inviolable. Thus, although job rotation or enrichment programs are introduced to relieve monotony and small areas of decision making are relinquished, the basic hierarchical structure of the organization is maintained. The socialist view, evident in some parts of Europe, assumes that individuals cannot develop fully because they have lost or have never had the necessary autonomy; to develop fully, they must gain control over their own work and, in one form or another, control over the entire enterprise.

The human relations approach in the United States has found strong support from managerial groups, who advocate the free enterprise system, and from unions. As A. H. Raskin (1975:1) commented, organized labor is "firmly wedded to the enterprise system—so firmly that it is still cold to any direct worker role in running business...." For the most part, when unions have chosen to join management in cooperative schemes, they have opted to serve in an advisory capacity. The reason for this position was expressed by Samuel Gompers in 1920. Although labor unions should properly be concerned with such questions as wages, hours, plant sanitary and safety conditions, and employee comfort, he maintained, wage earners should not expect to "assume control of industry," have "responsibility for financial management," or "usurp the rights of owners" (Gompers 1920:286). Thus, unions have traditionally believed that it is management's right and responsibility to manage and that unions will participate to achieve better working conditions, greater job security, and increased financial benefits.

This belief is based in part on the feeling that unions are in a conflicting position when they first assist in formulating policy and then later represent the employees in grieving about it. Because of the problems of taking both an opposing and a cooperative stance, unions often prefer to be critics rather than partners, disavowing formal responsibility for the organization's management, even while providing advice or assistance.

Support for a relatively limited role for employees in decision making can be found in the academic literature. S. Mallet has drawn a distinction between participation in management that involves making policy decisions and that which concerns matters of internal organization. He believes that when employees speak about managing the enterprise, they really mean managing their own work and they are not concerned about the far-reaching aims and purposes of their work (Roback 1970:8). Strauss and Rosenstein (1970:211) concur, adding that "worker representatives have neither the technical background nor the interest to concern themselves deeply with questions of finance, marketing, and the like....their interest is chiefly in the impact of shop-level changes." Derber (1970b:131) takes this position a step further, contending that as long as workers' economic and personal needs are satisfied, they are not strongly motivated to become involved in decision making at all.

Over the past two decades, however, these traditional views have been put to the test by such advocates of worker participation as Irving Bluestone, the retired vice president and head of the General Motors Department of the UAW. He maintains that improving the quality of work life means not only giving workers a participative role in managing their own work, but "ultimately even a participative role in managing certain aspects of the enterprise." He does concede that workers generally are more concerned with decisions that affect them immediately, but insists that when they come to realize that certain managerial functions can affect their welfare, they will want to participate in making decisions about them too (Bluestone 1974:27, 29).

By any gauge, however, it must be concluded that the type of decision-making responsibility that American employees have, the subjects over which they may exercise control, and the levels of the enterprise at which they are involved remain relatively limited in the 1980s. To see why this is the case, one must consider the subjects about which decisions are made in the firm.

Adolf Sturmthal (1968:25) has suggested five major areas of managerial decision making: (1) corporate finance, (2) personnel, (3) production, (4) procurement of outside contractors, and (5) technological change. A general list of subjects that become objects of decision making within the enterprise can be developed by combining topics included under these categories (see table 2).

Table 2
Decision-Making Topics in the Firm

1. Corporate Financing and General Policy

Financing of plant and equipment	Product selection
Reinvestment	Purchasing
General accounting procedures	Appointments to top managerial positions
Amortization of indebtedness	Opening and closing of units
Depreciation of plant and equipment	Plant location
Marketing and distribution	Incentive systems, profit sharing, and bonus plans
Long-term planning and development	Pension funds
Stock purchase	
Income guarantees	

2. Personnel

a. Wages and Conditions of Employment

Wages	Dismissal and severance pay
Fringe benefits	Work and shop rules
Rate structure and wage differentials	Safety and health
Individual and general wage adjustments	Grievances
Work schedules	Attendance and lateness
Job classification	Rest periods
Job evaluations	Physical conditions
Job transfers	Overtime regulations
Seniority systems	Leaves of absence
Discipline	
Shift transfers	*b. Manpower*
Promotion and upgrading	Hiring
Layoffs	Work force size
Attrition arrangements	Training, apprenticeship
	Employment stabilization
	Labor turnover

3. Production

Quality	Output standards
Tools	Utilization of machinery
Methods improvement	Plant layout
Production planning	Scheduling of operations
	Scrap reduction

4. Procurement

Subcontracting

5. Technological Change

Changes in job content	Retooling
Retraining	

Source: Gold 1976: 8.

Through their unions and the process of collective bargaining, employees have primarily been able to have a say in decisions affecting personnel matters. In addition, some analysts contend that "in principle no area of managerial decison making is completely and definitely removed from the scope of collective bargaining" (Sturmthal 1968:25). Labor and management, for example, may bargain over the issue of subcontracting even when there is no specific clause in the contract covering the subject, since decisions in the area of procurement have an impact on hiring, work force size, employment stabilization, work schedules, layoffs, and the like. In the final analysis, however, despite the presence of statutes that proscribe managerial discretion, there are significant areas of decision making in many firms in which management has the ultimate word and in which the union does not participate.

When it comes to joint committees (which are the creation of labor and management), these groups must carve out areas of decision making over which they will have responsibility. Some committees may consider issues that were not discussed extensively at the workplace before. But, for the most part, they are ceded certain areas of responsibility—by management, when it relinquishes traditional prerogatives and the right to make unilateral decisions about specific subjects; and by both unions and management, when subjects normally handled in collective negotiations are allowed to be discussed by joint committees. As to be expected, neither labor nor management has been willing to turn over major areas of decision making that will affect large groups of employees or the enterprise itself.

By far the greatest level of participation in U.S. firms takes place in the employee's immediate work area, where it is assumed that the employee's contribution can be the greatest and where a degree of autonomy is granted. The amount of decision-making autonomy given to employees, however, is by no means a settled issue. Stephen H. Fuller, a vice president of the General Motors Corporation, for example, raises some basic questions in this regard:

> Should control be viewed as external to the individual, as provided for through a supervisor and shop rules? Or should it lie within the individual's self-regulating ability and value system...? Moving from external to self-regulating sources of control would seem to be consistent with the quality-of-worklife view point. How much training and how much information is management willing to provide if employees are to be self-regulating? (Fuller 1980:39)

Conflicting Attitudes: Cooperation or Cooptation?

Little unanimity exists within the ranks of either labor or management as to the desirability or effectiveness of cooperative programs. Just as there are those who proseletize the process, so too are there those who deeply distrust it.

The Union Side

Opposition exists to programs that are intended to increase productivity, as well as to those that seek to improve working conditions through QWL activities. The less than enthusiastic approach among certain segments of the union movement to QWL projects can probably best be summarized in the statements of William W. Winpisinger, president of the International Association of Machinists and Aerospace Workers, who has criticized such programs as a management ploy that ultimately weakens labor unions and diverts attention from the basic, and essential, issues of wages, job security, and health and safety. Winpisinger is reported to have said, "If you want to enrich the job, enrich the pay check."

In 1976, Congressman Stanley N. Lundine (Dem., Jamestown, N.Y.) introduced the Human Resource Development Act, a bill calling for a "national commitment" to an economy of full employment and economic stabilization and advocating labor-management cooperation. At that time, the labor movement, along with others, withheld support for fear that enactment of the bill would preclude passage of the Humphrey-Hawkins bill, which was also before Congress. When Congressman Lundine introduced another version of the act in 1977, representatives of the Department of Labor testified that some provisions were redundant and that worker participation would not be effective without job security. Although it did not testify, the AFL-CIO, through Andrew J. Biemiller of its Legislative Department, prepared a statement that was circulated unofficially, stating that the bill was "a license for outsiders to muck about in the delicate balance of labor-management relations" (Leone 1983:179).

Robert W. Ahern of the Buffalo-Erie County Labor-Management Council, however, contends that although the statement was released, Mr. Biemiller adopted a neutral position shortly thereafter. According to Ahern (1983:205), "Currently, the position of the AFL-CIO, as I read the statements of Tom Donahue [secretary-treasurer] and even the fiesty Mr. Winpisinger is that they back labor-management cooperation as long as it is deeply embedded and controlled by the collective bargaining process. This keeps the process 'honest,' in Donahue's terms, and presumably prevents management from gaining the fruits of cooperation while 'mugging the union at the plant gate,' to use Winpisinger's colorful phrase." Above all, these union leaders are opposed to a process that undermines collective bargaining. Howard D. Samuel, president of the Industrial Union Department of the AFL-CIO, concludes that "mostly, it's a surface effort which frequently masks a corporate effort to dump collective bargaining obligations" (Serrin 1984:136).

The negative approach to cooperative programs is based in part on the view that the aims of such programs are "essentially motherhood goals." No one disputes the fact that conditions at work should be improved, but it is believed that that goal can best be achieved by "redoubling union efforts to obtain higher wages, shorter hours and improved benefit packages" (Hanlon 1981:9). Still other union leaders maintain that humanizing the workplace or making hierarchical relationships more democratic are secondary goals that can be considered only after basic issues of low wages and job insecurity are resolved.

Pessimism in certain sectors of the labor movement about the ability of these programs to increase productivity has also been long standing. Reaction to efforts to encourage increased productivity in the early 1970s, for example, was less than enthusiastic. In 1971, *Business Week* reported that when then Secretary of Labor James D. Hodgson appeared at the midsummer executive council meeting of the AFL-CIO in San Francisco to ask for labor's cooperation in increasing productivity, he received a cold reception. "[George] Meany objected to what he said was Hodgson's suggestion that labor productivity is slipping and that union members and the contracts regulating their work—the controversial work rules argued about in most big negotiations—are a cause of recent disturbing low productivity" (*Business Week* 1971:30).

Some common conceptions about what increased productivity entailed may have caused this initial reaction. *Business Week* implied a certain definition of growth in productivity in the following statement: "Employers worried about costs and forced to raise wages have been trying, in industry after industry, to change contracts to require more work and perhaps fewer employees, in return for more pay; few have made significant gains" (1971:30).

The now defunct National Commission on Productivity and Work Quality (NCPWQ) fought vigorously to alter this view. In a Harris poll the commission found that 67 percent of those interviewed agreed and only 20 percent disagreed with the statement that "companies benefit from increased productivity at the expense of workers" (NCPWQ 1973:12). In response to the question whether productivity should be considered a labor or management problem, John Stewart, the commission's executive director in 1973, replied that "most of the gains have come from things like changing management or technical practices; additional capital; education of the work force; mobility of labor; economies of scale.... it's not a labor or a management productivity problem. Depending on the industry and the technology, each has a role in improving it" (*Nation's Business* 1973:65).

In some unions, these same doubts persist today. In part, those opposing cooperative programs still believe that "unions have objectives directly at odds with those of management" and that, at best, all one may hope to attain is "antagonistic co-operation" (Dubin 1949:196-97). Opposition thus is based on some of the following assumptions:

- Economic benefits of cooperation accrue only to management.
- With increased physical productivity as the result of technological change, current employees will lose their jobs and the overall number of job opportunities in the plant or industry will be reduced.
- Partial involvement might well be a ploy to legitimize management decisions

without granting union members any real power. Thus, union members will be coopted.

- Union committee members will become alienated from their own constituents as they become involved with management's problems and perhaps even identify with management itself.

- Joint participation will undermine the union's ability to be militant in seeking economic gains at the bargaining table, and cooperation will be interpreted as a sign of bargaining weakness.

- The responsibility for increasing productivity and reducing costs lies with management rather than with labor.

A fear of cooptation was apparent even in what many conceded to be one of the more successful joint labor-management programs—the one functioning between the General Motors Corporation and the UAW. In 1981 GM sent a private memo to its executives throughout the country "urging them to use its quality-of-work-life program to persuade workers that union wage demands would harm the country." In 1984, in another private document, GM suggested that Donald Ephlin, then director of the UAW's Ford department, was more capable than most men of understanding GM's position in the forthcoming negotiations. A perception among rank and file members that Ephlin had become a "captive of management" (a perception disputed by others) contributed, according to several union officials, to his failure to win the UAW presidency in 1983 (Serrin 1984:137). (Ephlin was the UAW official responsible for negotiating the very novel Saturn plan, discussed at the conclusion of chapter 3.)

At the same time, however, support for cooperative efforts is also deeply rooted in certain sectors of the labor movement. As early as 1930, Samuel Gompers wrote, "The union is just as necessary for the new function—cooperation—as it is for defensive and bargaining purposes.... Cooperation comes with development and maturity" (quoted in Douty 1974:11).

In the early 1970s, despite some skepticism and in the face of shrinking business profits, rising inflation that curtailed buying power, and rising unemployment, some union leaders were "ready to accept management programs to improve productivity—including technological advances—provided they do not increase the employee work load, jeopardize workers' jobs, or produce more profits for the employer without giving employees a share of the gain" (*Business Week* 1972:100).

In the mid-1980s, there is growing support for the cooperative process within the labor movement. AFL-CIO President Lane Kirkland, for example, noted, "We still need the 'us versus them.' We do, after all, represent different interests. But it doesn't have to be a conspicuous exercise in class hostility" (Michaels 1984:15). And Martin D. Hanlon, in a study he describes as "the only one of its kind," sought the opinions of a diverse group of union leaders, management representatives, and employees who had been involved in QWL/cooperative projects. He came to the "most unexpected discovery" that union leaders were consistently the most enthusiastic supporters of their projects. "As a group, they held the most favorable opinions about...the labor-management committee, improvements in labor-management climate, and the project as a whole" (Hanlon 1981:11).

A strong and persistent voice favoring cooperative efforts is that of Irving Bluestone, formerly of the UAW, who continues to be an active spokesman on labor issues. His advocacy for such programs stems from his basic interest in humanizing the workplace. "My feeling was: Damn it, it's about time that workers were given more than just the opportunity to be order-takers. They're not adjuncts to the tool, they're not automatons, they're human beings. They've got to be treated with dignity and they've got to be given the opportunity to use their God-given ingenuity and powers to be creative themselves" (*QWL Review* 1981:17).

The Management Side

The expanding list of companies experimenting with or actively involved in cooperative programs attests to the fact that certain segments of the management community have been willing to keep an open mind about and have supported cooperative efforts. Conference Board president James T. Mills notes that there is currently a "reappraisal of the way U.S. work forces are managed. As a result of this examination, traditional assumptions about work, workers and the workplace are being questioned" (Gorlin and Schein 1984: v).

Initial resistance to joint activities in the 1970s was pervasive, with members of management displaying suspicion about union motives as well as concern about diminution of their own roles. In a survey of 563 managers, for example, it was found that 49 percent believed that unions were opposed to productivity improvements (Stepina 1982:8). Uppermost in many minds was the fear that employee participation would invade management rights. David W. Ewing, of the *Harvard Business Review*, said that "U.S. corporations are noted for many qualities and achievements but not for democratic methods of control and governance. Top executives habitually disdain the idea of 'popularity contests' as a vehicle of decision making" (Ewing 1971:24).

In 1971, the journal made a survey of 3,453 subscribers (primarily managers) and 185 Harvard Business School students. One-third of the respondents were willing to allow employees to vote on such policy issues confronting top management as plant relocation, mandatory retirement age, continuation of controversial defense contracts, company recruitment policies, and the assignment of individuals to new plants and offices. Sixty-one percent, however, indicated that management need not be bound by employee opinions. Forty-one percent of those who outright rejected employee participation in these matters were willing to consider balloting if it were limited to managerial groups (Ewing 1971:26-28).

In some management circles, resistance to joint committees has been based on some of the following assumptions (Gold 1974:12):

- Employee participation is likely to mean a loss of authority and prestige for management (that is, it is an invasion of management rights) and a concomitant buildup of strength and prestige for unions.
- Workers will not be able to contribute that much to management decision making because they are not acquainted with the intricate and complicated factors involved in running an enterprise.
- Participation will bypass middle management, inhibit its development, and weaken the staff function.
- The pace of decision making will be slowed and management responsibility and accountability diffused. Thus, needed technological change actually may be delayed and the goal of increased efficiency impaired.
- The union will be unwilling to give up make-work rules, a position reflected in a *Business Week* article (1972:100) stating, "restrictive [union] work rules and stubborn worker resistance to anything that looks like a speedup remain the greatest barriers to improving output per man-hour."

With the experience of the past ten years behind us, it is now possible to determine how the attitudes of managers who have worked in joint programs have changed—if at all. The results of the Conference Board's extensive study published in 1984 found that most executives queried believed that "the experience now being gained in participative management and quality-of-work-life efforts will yield a reliable alternative managerial style, necessary for the future of U.S. productivity," but that they have doubts and "uncertainties about current state-of-the-art practices" (Gorlin and Schein 1984:33-38).

Among the more negative comments that were made were the following:

- The participative style is too recent and too little understood; its adoption may be too abrupt in certain workplaces.
- These changes may be judged another management gimmick, another fad.
- The use of "innovations" is a mask for poor management.
- Innovations, especially problem-solving groups, have a limited life expectancy.
- The problem-solving process has too little influence on the organization to generate anything but short-term gains.

- Problem-solving groups require too much time for preparation and implementation and are not worth the return in cost savings.

- Middle management remains the greatest obstacle to securing acceptance and commitment to the new work plan. Many middle managers fear a loss of authority and power and are unprepared for the demands of a participative style.

- The union is a political institution whose officers will manipulate QWL issues in the union election process.

- Unions refuse to approve joint programs until they receive concessions in other areas.

- Unions impede open communication, which is fundamental to the implementation of the new programs.

Positive remarks include the following:

- Designs for group participation are long term in nature, offer substantial employee development, and can continue to generate new ideas in a wide variety of functional areas.

- Problem solving is an ongoing employee-development tool that will yield long-term benefits.

- Problem-solving groups are instruments for improving a work situation and are excellent communication devices.

- Improved communication and a stronger team effort lead to a greater consciousness of quality and productivity on the job.

- Joint programs lessen (but do not eliminate) natural tensions between labor and management.

- Joint programs improve the negotiation process (Gorlin and Schein 1984:33-38).

Third-Party Observers

Traditionally, in the literature, neutral third-party observers have tended to conclude that labor and management will be induced to join together only when they become aware that they are facing a mutual crisis. An industry, for example, may be confronted with increased competition from countries with lower labor costs, be dependent on expensive raw materials, face the need for modernization, and generally feel the effects of inflation and recession. At times such as these, people join together to overcome common obstacles. Once the crisis has ended, cooperative efforts end as well. Concern for the short-lived nature of these programs was expressed by managers in the Conference Board study who "wondered if the new and closer relationship would deteriorate with economic recovery" (Gorlin and Schein 1984:38).

There is also concern that cooperative efforts may not be sufficient to offset the effects of a crisis. The existing "market structure, potential demand for product, and the degree of monopolistic industrial organization" may be so adverse as to make it impossible for individuals working within the firm through joint committees to overcome these external problems (Davey 1968:8). Ernest Dale has pointed to the demise of many labor-management plans in the depression of 1930-33 because "losses were often so overwhelming that labor's contributions were insignificant in comparison." The industries in which committees have the best chance for success are those whose technology is already dynamic, but which would experience even greater growth if labor and management were to cooperate in raising productivity (in Davey 1968:8).

In the 1980s, Irving Bluestone was pleased to be able to report that QWL programs had continued during the depression in the automobile industry and that "even at a time when things were going to hell in a handbasket in the industry," there was "an even greater thrust to install programs of the QWL nature" (*QWL Review* 1981:17).

III

ESTIMATES OF SUCCESS

Evaluations of the effectiveness of labor-management committees were mixed in 1976. They continue to be so in the 1980s. One finds, however, that despite the relatively high mortality rate of these committees in the past and, on occasion, pessimistic prognoses for their continuation in the future, there remains a hearty band of ardent and enthusiastic supporters for the process.

Several criteria can be used to gauge the success of labor-management committees, including their longevity, the interest of the participants and of the general public, and the extent to which cooperative efforts have achieved the goals they set out to attain.

Longevity

Milton Derber, described by David Jenkins as one of the few expert observers who have reviewed the evidence concerning democratic management and found it wanting, is reported to have said that, while he personally liked the notion of worker participation, the fact that it was rarely adopted was poor testimony to its effectiveness. Harvard psychiatrist Robert Coles, on the other hand, has noted that "one generation's impracticality has a way of becoming another's urgent necessity" (Jenkins 1973:308-10).

Writing in 1949, Robert Dubin said that "evidence from a number of American case studies indicates that co-operation on production between union and company is likely to be short-lived." In 1968, Harold W. Davey agreed with Dubin that joint committees were apt to be formed during a crisis period—as in the case of a war or when a business was marginal and was faced with a question of survival—and would not last when conditions returned to normal (Dubin 1949:195; Davey 1968:6).

H. M. Douty (1974) collected data on three Bureau of Labor Statistics (BLS) studies of joint committees conducted in 1948, 1963-64, and 1973, which were designed to determine how many committees were currently in effect. In January 1948, the BLS sent 3,023 questionnaires to plants that, according to the War Production Board, had joint committees operating in July 1945. The purpose of the questionnaires was to see how many joint committees had lasted into the postwar period. Of the 1,272 returns, 944 were usable. (It was assumed that, for the most part, those plants that failed to answer or returned unusable questionnaires had no committees.)

The findings showed that there were committees still operating in 287 plants—77 percent dealing with production problems, 69 percent with improving work quality, 57 percent with care of tools and equipment, 64 percent with absenteeism, and 84 percent with safety. Of the 457 plants reporting that joint committees had discontinued, the most common reasons given were the end of the war, ineffectiveness, and lack of interest. Seventy-one percent of the plants surveyed had fewer than a thousand workers. Two hundred twenty-three were unionized (Douty 1974:28-29).

The 1963-64 study analyzed 1,773 major collective bargaining agreements (defined as those covering a thousand employees or more) in effect during these two years. Agreements covering the railroads, airlines, and the government were excluded from the survey. Roughly a quarter (450) had union-management cooperation provisions, but only 92 had labor-management committees. Forty-four of these joint committees dealt with production problems.

The 1973 study covered the same groups, but in this case the contracts numbered 1,311. Here only 64 called for joint productivity committees. (Douty assumed that since the majority of committees in the 1948 study were in plants with fewer than a thousand workers, some of which were nonunionized, the figures for 1963-64 and 1973, which covered only unionized plants with more than a thousand employees, might be somewhat misleading.) Douty concluded in 1974 that "joint production committees are not widely used to promote efficiency in industry or the public service" (Douty 1974:34).

In 1980, Paul S. Goodman's study (Schuster 1983:193) of QWL projects with at least five years' experience found that 75 percent of them were no longer functioning and that none of those he considered in a unionized setting was in operation. In a second study conducted over a four- to seven-year period and published in 1983, Michael Schuster reported similar findings in his analysis of the life cycle of ten plant "interventions."

> The first four to be terminated were L-MCs. One L-MC never started although it was contained in the parties' national agreement; a second died after six months. In both instances there was no real commitment to change by either party. In the third case, the parties met often but never had the internal expertise to get the process moving, nor the wisdom to seek outside assistance. This venture terminated after two years. In the fourth case, the L-MC process led to a recommendation to implement autonomous work groups, a proposal that caused a severe division within both the local union's leadership and its membership, and was overwhelmingly defeated.
>
> Three productivity sharing plans ended—one after three years and the other two after six years each. In all three instances, errors in judgment by management led to the perception that the bonus formula had been manipulated. In the latter two cases, 18-week strikes occurred, in part due to the productivity sharing plan. The record is only three out of ten interventions surviving after six years. It is important to note, however, that the three remaining efforts are successful after 8, 12, and 27 years, respectively (Schuster 1983:193-94).

CWA president Glenn Watts suggests that those programs that have failed may have been "narrow participation programs," which offer nothing to workers in the long run "beyond promises and rhetoric." Speaking disparagingly of quality circles, he endorsed another type of QWL—"one which involves a serious and long-term change in management style, based on a philosophy of trust and respect for employees" (Watts 1983:12).

Perhaps the most graphic way to evaluate what has happened to cooperative programs in the past decade or so is to look at some of those programs discussed in our 1976 report and see where they are today, as well as to consider one or two other programs of interest.

Mining

In 1973, United Mine Workers president Arnold Miller provided high-level endorsement for the initiation of a cooperative program at a Pennsylvania coal mining company with approximately 190 employees. All workers in an experimental section were paid at the highest possible rate and the section decided where it would work each day. Anyone in the section could run any piece of equipment. Grievances were handled through the normal channels, but representatives from labor and management first met in an attempt to solve problems before going through the grievance process. The company found that the average rate of absenteeism was reduced from 4.5 percent to 1.5 percent, the company experienced the highest rate of productivity in the experimental section it had ever achieved, the number of federal and state violations of safety regulations was down from fourteen to four, and the crew members were increasingly enthusiastic about the new system.

After implementing this successful pilot project in one section of the mine, it was extended to the entire mine. Results there too were generally favorable in terms of productivity and worker satisfaction. But despite positive evaluations, "local union members rejected continuation of the plan after a two-year trial. One of the reasons for the rejection was fear of 'union busting.' This fear was felt by 'quite a number of union members, including some of the most influential older workers' " (Stepina 1982:7).

The Auto Industry

In 1976, we wrote that a second program combining a quality of work approach and an active labor-management committee was in progress in Harman International Industries in Bolivar, Tennessee, a company that produced car mirrors and was organized by the UAW. This program was worked out by Irving Bluestone, then vice president of the UAW, and Sidney Harman, then president of the corporation. It functioned with a plantwide committee composed of five representatives each from labor and management and smaller subcommittees to channel information from the work force. Among the goals of the program were greater job protection and security and an equitable division of job responsibilities. Although representatives from labor and management concluded that there had been some improvement in productivity, increased productivity was not the primary goal of the program. Rather, it was to create better working conditions where there is less stress and an improvement in morale (Gold 1976:24).

Asked about the program in 1980, Bluestone remarked,

> It's unfortunate that it was given so much publicity. These experiments get too much publicity in the initial stages before you know whether or not they will be successful.
>
> That program was coming along well. It received its impetus from an understanding that Sid Harman, who was then Chairman of the Board of Harman Industries, and I had worked out. When Harman left to join the Carter Administration in the Department of Commerce, he sold his interest in the firm to a large conglomerate, Beatrice Foods. Beatrice Foods indicated that it was interested but obviously it was not committed. The result was that the program went into an hiatus position.
>
> The level to which it had moved in the previous years remained. All of the aspects of the program, which had developed over a period from 1972 until 1976 or 1977 are still intact. However, it reached a plateau after Beatrice Foods lost interest. And as a result, it's just stuck there and for the present, frankly, I don't see that it's going to move off that dead-center.
>
> The one thing about such a program that's interesting is that once the workers have the taste of what this improvement in the quality of their worklife can mean for them, they won't let go of it. So, under Beatrice Foods, no more progress has been made, but neither has the company dared to take away from the workers that which they had already gained by reason of the program. So they get that benefit but it hasn't gone further (*QWL Review* 1981:15).

In 1973, in the course of bargaining for a new national agreement, General Motors Corporation and the UAW agreed to establish a National Joint Committee to Improve the Quality of Worklife and urged their local managements and unions to cooperate in experiments and projects. By 1980, over ninety such projects were underway in nearly all plants (*QWL Review* 1981:17).

The programs, which vary from plant to plant, are all based on the following premise:

- There will be no loss of jobs as a result of the program (although layoffs due to business cycles may be inevitable).

- Provisions of the national and local agreements are inviolable.
- Participation is voluntary.
- Union and management representatives are involved in all aspects of the program.
- Either party may withdraw at any time (Bluestone 1980:40).

Under this arrangement, no separate QWL committees are formed. The local union shop committee is the union counterpart. Periodic plant and team meetings are used to air problems and to discuss such aspects of the business as quality, schedules, scrap and rework, housekeeping, safety, employee facilities, production facilities, and customer orders. Training is also an essential component, designed to aid employees in acquiring knowledge and skills (Bluestone 1980:40).

At one plant, the traditional structure was abandoned and the plant was divided into six business teams, covering engineering scheduling, material handling, quality control, maintenance, and accounting. Support employees became an integral part of the operation. Through quality circles, employees met regularly to discuss problems affecting the work environment and the plant's performance (Fuller 1980:30).

Steel

The following discussion of the 1971-74 activities of labor-management committees in the steel industry is from Gold (1976:28-30); sources of information were Abel (1974:1-9), Thrasher (1973:12-16), *Business Week* (1971:58), and *U.S. News and World Report* (1973:120).

In 1971, the United States, producing 120.2 million tons of steel, slipped to second place (Russia produced 132 million tons) as the world' largest steel producer, a rank it had held since 1895. As a consequence of the problems in the industry, the United Steelworkers (USW) joined with the steel companies in the 1971 basic steel negotiations to include a provision establishing joint advisory committees on productivity at every plant covered by the contract. At the start of December 1971, international officials met with local officers in a series of five regional meetings to issue guidelines and encourage the formation of the committees in local plants. In certain areas, such as Pittsburgh, where the industry was operating at about 50 percent capacity, the USW told local leaders to begin with an educational campaign directed at the members and wait until operations rose above 70 percent before starting up the committees.

By the first part of 1973, approximately 200 mills had functioning labor-management committees; in the latter part of 1974, the number had risen to about 250. By May 1973, nearly three thousand meetings had been held. Most of the committees met monthly, although in some places formal meetings were conducted quarterly, with more informal sessions taking place more frequently. The USW generally proposed the establishment of a plant-level joint productivity committee to serve as a steering committee, with subcommittees operating in plant departments.

Guidelines for the plantwide committees specified that the union would be represented by the local union president, chairman of the grievance committee, secretary of the grievance committee, and a "rotating" member of the grievance committee to represent a special area of any department whose problems were to be discussed during a particular month. The company was to be represented by the plant superintendent or manager (or designated representative), plant manager of labor relations, plant industrial engineer, and a "rotating" department superintendent. In addition, a union staff representative from the international could be invited to attend monthly meetings to consult and advise the local union members.

An essential tenet of the committee was that it was in no way to interfere with existing rights of the parties under the provisions of the basic labor agreement. If either party felt that a proposed action would violate the contract in meetings of the various subcommittees, they were to convey this concern to the plant-level committee for its evaluation before proceeding. It was suggested that the parties submit an agenda in advance of each session indicating topics to be discussed. The union participants were to serve solely in an advisory capacity to management.

The aims of the committees were fivefold: improve productivity, promote orderly relations in the plants to ensure uninterrupted operation, promote the use of domestic steel, encourage company progress and thus worker prosperity, and review issues of special concern to the parties. Among these issues might be more efficient use of time and facilities, the reduction of breakdowns and delays, improving quality control, eliminating waste, reducing overtime, increasing employee morale, improving worker safety, and educating employees to the need for greater productivity and the threat of foreign competition—through plant open houses, movies, slide presentations, trips to customers' plants, and the like.

The benefit to the employee was that increased productivity would serve as "the basis for future wage increases and continued job security" (Abel 1974:9). Steelworkers president I. W. Abel was quoted as saying in 1971, "You know as well as I you cannot go to a well that's gone dry and get a bucket of water" (Thrasher 1973:12). The companies would benefit when increased productivity offset cost increases.

Abel reported that, as of 1973, the steel industry had raised production, increased productivity, and changed the trend of imports and exports. The contract resulting from the 1974 basic steel negotiations, however, called for a new Industry-Union Employment Security and Plant Productivity Committee at the industry level to review and coordinate plant activities, giving special attention to those plants with lagging productivity. Abel conceded that progress had varied considerably among plants, with some committees showing indifference, a lack of cooperation, and, on occasion, refusing to meet.

Lee P. Stepina (1982:7) reported that indeed many union members had questioned the benefits of the cooperation plan. They felt that it was merely a management tool for controlling the union. "In a campaign marked by charges of 'selling out to management,' the USW's incumbent president I. W. Abel's hand chosen candidate Lloyd McBride won a very narrow victory over challenger Ed Sadlowski. McBride asumed office in 1977 and quickly killed the cooperation plan."

According to Sam Camens, assistant to the president of the Steelworkers, the history of the Joint Advisory Committee on Productivity begun in 1971 shows that it was a total failure. Among the reasons for its lack of success were that: (1) it was strictly a productivity committee and not concerned with workplace improvement; (2) it was purely advisory in nature and the union truly had no real input on an equal basis; (3) it did not have the backing of local unions and was not on a voluntary basis, where joint input has genuine mutual backing; (4) it did not even discuss root causes of worker alienation and made no attempt to change employee-employer relationships, or improve union-company relationships; (5) it was a top-heavy committee that included only plant supervision and local union officers, with no input from plant floor representatives; (6) it increased worker mistrust of management (Camens 1982:6-7).

In 1980, however, labor-management cooperation in the industry was brought back to life. In April of that year, the United Steelworkers and the Coordinating Committee Steel Companies (Basic Steel Industry) signed a Labor-Management Participation Teams Experimental Agreement. The agreement became effective on August 1, 1980. This program, Camens maintains, could "be a major contributing factor to job security and [could] improve productivity in the steel industry (1982:2). Proponents of the concept believed that in time and with proper training, the voluntary joint problem-solving plant floor teams that were to be developed could implement changes in the quality of products, production methods, equipment, and environment and working conditions "that would substantially improve the total industrial process and relations" (1982:7). By 1982, the program was in effect in thirteen plants operated by Bethlehem, Jones & Laughlin, National, Republic, and U.S. Steel, with approximately one hundred teams organized.

In this program, a participation committee is set up at the plant level to coordinate the activities of departmental or unit level participation teams. These, in turn, are composed of management and employee cochairmen and employee and supervisory members of the department. Employee members are paid for time away from work at their average straight time rate. Team members are free to discuss, consider, and decide on proposed ways to improve department or unit performance, employee morale and dignity, and conditions of the work site. Appropriate subjects include use of production facilities, quality of products and of the work environment, safety and environmental health, scheduling and reporting arrangements, absenteeism and overtime, incentive coverage and yield, job alignments, contracting out, and energy conservation and transportation pools. The committees and teams have no jurisdiction over grievances and no authority to add to, detract from, or change the terms of the basic labor agreement (Camens 1982:4-5).

Camens describes the list of problems addressed by a team of maintenance employees at Jones & Laughlin Steel's Hennepin Plant in Illinois as typical of the issues considered by these groups. Two percent dealt exclusively with employee convenience (food machines); 7 percent with employee relations; 4.5 percent with employee scheduling; and 84 percent with production, maintenance, and quality. Specific solutions arrived at by team members in various plants include the following:

- Development of a tool availability program on a blast furnace cast house at a cost of $16,000, which saved $330,000 per year in furnace delay production.
- Development of a standard operating procedure to stop excess rolling for each order on a cold mill, for a cost savings of $713,043 per year.
- Extension of a runway and reorganization of a roll rack area to alleviate rust damage caused by water dripping into a coil area. Savings amounted to $11,680 per year.
- Changes in the rolling mill hot bed and rolling procedure to eliminate camber in steel billets. Potential savings are in the millions of dollars (Camens 1982:11-14).

The Federal and Public Sectors

A plan, which Milton Derber termed "an unusually harmonious system of industrial government," went into effect in 1940 with the first signed contract for manual workers at the Tennessee Valley Authority (TVA), a public agency operated along the lines of a private enterprise. The agreement set up joint cooperative committees designed to "eliminate waste, conserve materials, improve workmanship, promote education and training, correct conditions making for grievances and misunderstanding, safeguard health, prevent hazards to life and property, better employment conditions, and strengthen morale" (Derber 1970:332). Cooperative committees function at a systemwide level and in each plant. Suggestions are processed by the committees from both labor and management. Throughout the years, there has been a steady increase in the number of suggestions per employee and the percentage dealing with labor saving ideas (Stepina 1982:7).

Stepina (1982) concluded that TVA management fully accepted and supported this program because TVA management had been born in the Depression and because of its status as a public body. "This combination of labor needs and management philosophy resulted in a successful plan." He found, however, that "because the TVA is an agency of the federal government paying prevailing wages, it may not be a representative case."

Examples of other programs in the federal sector include a labor-management committee at the Indian School in Flandreau, South Dakota, begun in 1978 by the Bureau of Indian Affairs and the National Federation of Federal Employees, and another at the Veterans Medical Center in Pittsburgh, involving the hospital and the American Federation of Government Employees, begun in 1975.

Just as the first labor-management cooperative program in the steel industry was adjudged to be a failure and then later reconstituted, so too was the citywide Joint Labor-Management Productivity Committee in New York City. A study by Anna C. Goldoff (1978) evaluated the effectiveness of the committee, which was established in 1976 and was composed of equal numbers of representatives from the city and the Municipal Labor Committee. The program grew out of the city's financial crisis— specifically, from an agreement signed by the municipal unions and the city. The agreement reflected conditions set for federal seasonal loans by the State Emergency Financial Control Board and by then Secretary of the Treasury William Simon. It was agreed that no municipal employees would receive cost-of-living adjustments unless there were matched productivity savings. Those savings could not be achieved through service reductions or changes in contract items.

The committee's function was to guide and approve the work of twenty-six agency subcommittees. The subcommittees, in turn, were cochaired by union and management and had an equal number of representatives from each side. Based on interviews with fifteen agency and twenty-one union representatives, Goldoff predicted that a long-term productivity program would not result from this effort.

> This research suggests that the participants in New York's productivity program are committed only to a short-term cash savings program to pay employee cost-of-living adjustments. Negative perceptions of future goal achievement, a diminishing environmental stimulus, and jurisdictional ambiguity between productivity and collective bargaining issues indicate that a long-term productivity program would not succeed.
>
> One obstacle is strong union dissatisfaction. Two-thirds of union respondents believed that the current program will disband after the agreement expires. In fact, 73 percent of the labor cochairmen interviewed agreed that the program will be unnecessary when normal collective bargaining is resumed. Because these cochairmen are local union leaders, their dissatisfaction and lack of commitment are definite weaknesses in the current program. Their negative perceptions will affect other labor participants in the program, as well as the union's rank and file (Goldoff 1978:33-34).

Abandoned during the Abraham Beame administration, the program was revived under Mayor Edward I. Koch. His first deputy mayor cochairs the committee, together with the president of District Council 37 of the American Federation of State, County and Municipal Employees (AFSCME). Representatives of the police, sanitation workers, firefighters, and communication workers unions serve on the committee, along with key city directors (operations, personnel, labor relations) and an observer from the Financial Control Board. According to Alan R. Viani, deputy chairman of the Office of Collective Bargaining in New York City, the committee no longer operates "on the basis of a price tag." (The city has now paid off its federal loans.) While activities of the committee result in cost savings in government, the program is not evaluated in monetary terms (conversation with author, February 25, 1986).

Joint labor-management committees function in ten or eleven mayoral agencies. Among the issues that have been considered by participants are alternate work schedules (compressed work weeks, staggered or flexible working hours), which have proven effective in reducing absenteeism; employee recognition programs; work site improvement projects, which deal with factors other than safety, designed to improve productivity; and employee assistance programs.

Among the major achievements of the program cited by Viani is a new citywide approach to computerizing payroll records, which has generated useful employment data and has reduced grievances over pay issues; the development of standards to govern subcontracting; and the creation of a health and accident information system to keep track of accidents and injuries on the job. Extensive training has also been conducted for employees. Viani believes that what is required at this juncture is an infusion of fresh, new ideas for projects on which the committee can work (conversation with author, February 25, 1986).

Another earlier effort at labor-management cooperation in the New York police department was short-lived. Three committees were established in 1971 by agreements between the department and the Sergeant's Benevolent Association, the Detective's Endowment Association, and the Lieutenant's Benevolent Association. Stepina (1982) found that "neither labor nor management was committed to committee decision making. Thus, management did not even participate in the committees. The sergeant's committee never met, and the other two met once or twice. Recommendations made by the two committees were totally rejected by the Police Commissioner. Not surprisingly, the committees were abandoned in 1972." That same year, the department negotiated an agreement with the Patrolmen's Benevolent Association (PBA) to set up a joint productivity committee to recommend experimental programs to improve the use of police personnel. The committee recommended a pilot program that was acceptable to management, but was turned down by the employees. The productivity clause became an issue in the PBA's elections just before the 1974 negotiations. The challenger defeated the president of the PBA who had negotiated the clause, and it was subsequently dropped in negotiations (Stepina 1982:8).

Other municipal programs include committees in Trenton, New Jersey, with AFSCME; in Cincinnati, between AFSCME and the Division of Highway Maintenance; and in Seattle, with the Metropolitan Seattle Transit District and the Amalgamated Transit Union.

Productivity Gain Sharing Plans

A brief word is in order about the longevity of gain sharing plans. A study conducted in 1973 found that Scanlon Plans enjoy a better success rate than similar programs. In a review of fifty-four cases, there were forty long-term successes and fourteen failures (Stepina 1982:7).

Members of management involved in gain sharing plans who responded to the Conference Board survey in 1984 believed that participation could not be sustained in the long run without sharing in productivity gains. They found that the program was essentially cost free, since bonuses are paid on the basis of increased production over and above a norm. A Motorola executive, for example, commented, "A combination of a participation-management environment and an incentive feature for productivity improvement is the best of both worlds" (Gorlin and Schein 1984:36).

In general, however, the Conference Board study found that outside of formal gain sharing plans, such as Scanlon, Rucker, and Improshare, the prevailing practice is not to offer bonuses for cost-savings solutions or increased productivity. Management representatives uniformly reject the notion, preferring instead nonmonetary recognition on a group basis. Among the reasons are the following:

- Work, when challenging and satisfying, as well as participation itself, is its own reward.
- The linking of monetary incentives to cost savings diminishes the spirit of participation and team building.
- Ideas and solutions may not be immediately or directly cost-efficient and may actually incur expenses.
- Economic stability and job security are sufficient motivators (Gorlin and Schein 1984:36-37).

Public Interest

Following unsuccessful efforts to gain federal support for labor-management cooperative programs in 1976 and 1977, Congressman Stanley N. Lundine saw the provisions of his Human Resource Development Act added as a rider to the Comprehensive Employment Training Act in 1978. The Federal Mediation and Conciliation Service (FMCS) was charged with implementing this self-contained piece of legislation, known as the Labor-Management Cooperation Act of 1978. Although fund levels were authorized for 1979 and 1980, it was not until 1981, after extensive lobbying, that appropriations were ultimately made (Leone 1983:180).

In its brochure describing the program, FMCS notes that it was the intent of the legislation that funds be awarded to support efforts of employees and employers covered by formal collective bargaining agreements. Committees receiving support are not limited to any particular activity, but have generally focused on improving labor relations, increasing productivity, and enhancing the quality of work life.

In 1981, FMCS awarded $999,856 to fourteen organizations (plant, area, and industry committees); in 1982 it gave $500,000 to seven groups; in 1983, it granted $486,252 to eight, all area labor-management committees. In 1984, prospects for continued federal appropriations were not good, with the Reagan administration indicating an interest in terminating the program. Lundine, however, pledged a major effort to obtain $2 million to continue its operation. He noted that he had originally envisioned a $10 million annual budget for cooperative projects, an amount that would still be five to six times less than that spent by other industrialized nations (*Daily Labor Report* 1983:A-1).

At the same time, however, the Office of Labor-Management Services in the U.S. Department of Labor was reconstituted in 1984 as the Bureau of Labor-Management Relations and Cooperative Programs. Previously a unit of the Labor-Management Services Administration, the bureau is now a separate agency of the Office of the Under Secretary.

Its principal aim is to encourage and assist employers, unions, and various third-party organizations to develop "more harmonious and mutually beneficial relationships." Ronald J. St. Cyr, then Acting Deputy Under Secretary for Labor-Management Relations and Cooperative Programs, wrote: "Specifically, it is our purpose to help devise ways of performing work under conditions that enhance both organizational effectiveness and a high quality of working life" (letter to the author, August 30, 1984).

In 1986, the continuing interest of FMCS and the Department of Labor in joint labor-management was evidenced by the convening of the Third National Labor-Management Conference in Washington, D.C., sponsored by these two organizations together with the National Association of Area Labor-Management Committees. Joining them in planning the conference were the AFL-CIO, AFSCME, Airline Industrial Relations Conference, American Arbitration Association, American Productivity Center, Industrial Relations Research Association, Maryland Center for Productivity and QWL, National Association of Manufacturers, National Mediation Board, National Public Employers Labor Relations Association, National Railway Labor Conference, and the Society of Professionals in Dispute Resolution (FMCS announcement, February 1986).

Committee Goals

There are many underlying assumptions in the argument for the development of labor-management committees. One of the most prominent is that employee participation will lead to greater productivity. To assess the precise value of participation in this respect, however, is difficult.

In a major study of labor-management cooperation during World War II, de Schweinitz, for example, attested to the fact that many labor and management officials felt that cooperation had added to the quantity and quality of production, but she could find no precise measures of productivity stemming from labor-management production committees (Douty 1974:28-29).

It is not that standards of productivity do not exist, but rather that there are problems in isolating the part that participation and cooperation play in increasing productivity. Leon Greenberg, the former executive director of the National Commission on Productivity and Work Quality, noted in 1973 that productivity is "the ratio of some measure of output to some measure of input." Total productivity, however, rests on the combined effect of a number of factors. In company productivity ratios, for instance,

> each ratio is influenced by the volume and quality of the other inputs employed and how effectively they are used. Output per man-hour, output per unit of capital, and output per unit of labor plus capital are all influenced by the volume of capital equipment, its stage of technological development, the quality and availability of materials, the scale of operations and rate of capacity utilization, organization and workflow, and other factors—as well as the very important contribution of the skill and attitude of the work force, including management (Greenberg 1973:2).

The labor components in many productivity ratios are usually man-hours paid for and man-hours worked. In some more sophisticated ratios, the quality of employment—due to different occupational levels or to differences in age, sex, or education—is weighted so that a measure of productivity can be constructed to take account of changes in skill requirements and occupational structure (Greenberg 1973:47-48).

In a further elaboration of this scheme—and in an effort to measure more accurately the profitability of participation—William C. Pyle of the Institute for Social Research at the University of Michigan studied "human resource accounting," computing figures for "(1) the value of investments in human resources (approximately corresponding to book value for physical assets); (2) replacement values; and (3) economic values, that is, the capitalized value of earnings directly attributable to these resources" (Jenkins 1973:239). With some of these measures, it was hoped that managers could evaluate the real costs of such things as training programs and employee turnover.

Earlier, however, Victor H. Vroom (1964:226) concluded that "when the entire pattern of results is considered, we find substantial basis for the belief that participation in decision making increases productivity. There is experimental and correlational evidence indicating that higher levels of influence by workers in making decisions that they are to carry out result in higher productivity than lower levels of influence." He added, however, that this is not always the case. Higher productivity could also be achieved using more autocratic methods.

Vroom also believed that there were no guarantees that decisions reached democratically would be better than those handed down autocratically. Much, he thought, would depend on whether management and labor were able to judge the organizational consequences of their decisions and whether these decisions were in harmony with organizational objectives.

Productivity is also dependent on how rapidly a decision is carried out, he contended. He found that participation affects whether a decision will be effectively implemented. "A high quality decision which is opposed by those expected to carry it out may result in lower productivity than a lower quality decision which is enthusiastically endorsed" (Vroom 1964:228).

Jenkins, a firm supporter of labor participation, while admitting that the evidence on productivity is not always clear-cut, finds that where it does exist, it shows that democratic participation is not inferior to traditional management methods in terms of financial consequences. "Somewhat primitive democratic systems" function as well or slightly better than orthodox systems and in companies in Britain, Scandinavia, and the United States where more scientific methods have been used, the results, he claims, are startling. Jenkins cites numerous examples where different forms of worker participation in the United States (usually in cases where individual workers have a great deal of personal discretion) has led to increased productivity—in terms of less employee turnover, fewer daily absences, employee earnings above standard, higher return on capital invested, and the like (Jenkins 1973:6).

Daniel Bell expresses greater certainty that democratic methods are not more profitable than conventional ones. He labels the suggestion as "hogwash" and attributes any superior results to a Hawthorne effect, in which productivity improves temporarily because workers are aware that they are the object of a scientific investigation (Jenkins 1973:309).

Respondents in the 1984 Conference Board study were reluctant to judge the results of their cooperative programs in monetary terms, believing that many aspects of the new relationships were not quantifiable. They felt that some of those elements that could be measured may have been due to factors other than a particular innovation. They believed that it is difficult to distinguish the part that a new program might play in increasing productivity, quality, or profitability, as opposed to that played by increased capital investment in new equipment, improved marketing, or better arrangements with suppliers. They also thought that such programs are a part of a long-term developmental process and that long-term results in terms of strengthening team effort may be incalculable (Gorlin and Schein 1984:33).

The fact remains, however, that productivity gains and other improvements are measured in cooperative programs. Among other elements also considered are reductions in absenteeism, accidents, and grievances; impact on collective bargaining relationships; and overall job satisfaction.

In 1983, FMCS issued a summary of preliminary results of labor-management cooperation programs. Among inplant committee programs it had supported, it found the following results:

- Diamond International Corporation: 18.7 percent increase in productivity; 30 percent decrease in absenteeism; 55 percent decrease in grievances; 40 percent decrease in quality-related mistakes; 48 percent decrease in disciplinary actions; two hundred fewer lost-time days per year.

- Rome Cable Corporation: 40 percent decrease in grievances; 16 percent decrease in accidents.

- Rath Packing Company: 31 percent decrease in absenteeism (expected to yield $1.27 million in annual productivity savings); $247,000 savings in annual overtime costs due to employee suggestions regarding the merger of three departments (*Daily Labor Report* 1983:D-1).

Among Scanlon Plans, the Parker Pen Company found that it was able to provide a 13 percent annual bonus to participants over a twenty-two-year period. In 1982, the company's manager of labor relations estimated a 100 percent productivity improvement over the previous ten years (Stepina 1982:7).

In addition to their impact on reducing formal grievances, cooperative programs are also said to have a positive effect on labor relations in general. Asked whether New York State's commitment to labor-management committees made negotiations any easier, Thomas F. Hartnett, director of the Governor's Office of Employee Relations, said,

> I think so, and I think the union negotiators think so as well. The kind of constructive dialogue created during the '78-'82 agreement made the collective bargaining process in '82 much smoother. Both sides went to the table with more credibility than in the past, because during the term of the previous agreement, as problems came up they were resolved. They may involve productivity, employee morale, or the ability to deliver services. Instead of waiting for negotiations, joint committees have stepped in and done some rather effective work in those areas. As a result, we've been able to defuse a lot of issues before they even got to the table (Hartnett 1982:13).

Irving Bluestone (1980:40-41) found ample evidence that the introduction of QWL programs had a positive impact on the usually adversarial collective bargaining process. He discovered, for example, that when the local parties in the UAW and GM were negotiating local issues in 1979 , all of the first ninety local settlements were accomplished without a strike threat. In forty-four of the ninety settlements, the parties were engaged in some type of QWL program.

In the 1984 Conference Board study, researchers found that "where formal labor-management agreements are in force, both company and union leaders note that the traditional adversary relationship of the two parties has been modified but not eliminated." They also concluded that in almost all situations, there were easier negotiations due to the new participative approach (Gorlin and Schein 1984:11).

When it comes to evaluating the effectiveness of cooperative programs in improving job satisfaction, the task becomes more difficult. A major assumption underlying the argument for labor-management committees is that participation will lead to more satisfied, happier employees. It is also assumed that increased job satisfaction, in turn, will result in (1) greater motivation and (2) higher productivity, and that participation will ensure better decision making (and thus produce greater efficiency).

Often in this area, one is reduced to relying on anecdotal material. In 1981, for example, at the Ford Motor Company's Green Island, New York, radiator and heater core plant, UAW Local 930 and the plant's management instituted what has been termed "one of the most active and successful employee involvement or quality of work life programs in the U.S. automobile industry." One employee noted that before the program began, morale and general employee attitudes were poor: "We sent junk out the door and collected our pay check. Nobody cared." Now, according to Ray Gongoleski, a fork-lift operator who serves as a part-time employee involvement coordinator, "The enthusiasm is incredible. We have people who are on layoff or on vacation who come in because they don't want to miss the meeting. We've gotten calls from the hospital. A man in for cardiac problems called in to apologize that he couldn't make the meeting" (*QWL Review* 1983:16).

Overcoming Barriers to Cooperation

In considering why certain cooperative programs were less successful than others, Conference Board researchers found a number of characteristics that appeared to contribute to a lack of success.

- The units with poor records were those in which there were severe management problems and poor profitability prior to the new plan.

- Union participation was either not invited early enough or was not invited at all.

- Real commitment from management (plant and/or corporate) was not communicated and proved.

- Training for managers, advisers, facilitators, and participants was insufficient.

- Line managers and supervisors did not fully accept their new roles in the participative environment.

- People were not convinced that gains in productivity would not lead to layoffs (Gorlin and Schein 1984:33-34).

Many of the suggestions for successful operation of labor-management committees have addressed the drawbacks raised by both labor and management. Several analysts, for instance, have thought that unions must have union security and be assured of their continuation. At the same time, they must maintain safeguards for current employees, so that improvements in productivity will not mean a loss of jobs. Management, on the other hand, must not be overly restricted in its ability to innovate, especially in relation to determining how jobs will get done. A constructive approach to work rules has to be adopted, taking into account the needs of each.

A general premise in the literature is that labor-management committees are best instituted with strong support from both top management and top union officials, as well as with the broad support of the rank and file. Middle management must also be involved. First-line supervisors may not change the way they supervise unless they receive strong support from their direct supervisors.

A union representative in the Conference Board study concluded that lack of progress in many QWL programs is attributable to competitive pressures among managers and supervisors and is due to the failure of companies to provide suitable support and rewards for nonauthoritarian managerial style. Many experts believe that earlier and more intensive preparation of middle- and lower-level managers for change in the organization is required, as is more attention to developing techniques to identify supervisors and managers with the potential for managing participatively (Gorlin and Schein 1984:37).

Some industrial relations specialists suggest that committees will succeed where industrial relations are already mature. This presupposes management's acceptance of collective bargaining and the absence of numerous grievances. Others maintain that there must be a fairly equal balance of power between the two groups, with the union being relatively stable and having made sufficient gains in negotiations to be in a position to make possible compromises.

Todd D. Jick, Robert McKersie, and Leonard Greenhalgh (1983:185-86) note that by far the most serious barrier to joint problem solving is the pervasive influence of adversarial norms, values, and practices. Behavior appropriate for successful negotiations is rarely appropriate for joint problem solving. In addition, because problem solving does not entail the same pressures and deadlines inherent in bargaining, the process is viewed as "soft" and capable of producing only limited gains. The techniques they propose for overcoming obstacles are shown in table 3.

Table 3

Techniques for Managing Typical Obstacles to Problem-Solving

Obstacles to Problem-Solving	Techniques for Enhancing Problem-Solving
1. Short-run orientation.	1. Introduce efforts to widen time-horizon.
2. Insufficient commitment by leaders to problem-solving.	2. Enhance affiliation with the process. Team building.
3. Intraorganizational counter-demands and role conflicts.	3. Preserve and fortify relations with principals and constituents. Credit parties with results. Use chairperson in mediator role within primary organizations.
4. Domination of the adversary system.	4. Keep distributive channels open for handling spillovers and conflict. Insulate the problem-solving process. Differentiate problem-solving from bargaining roles.

Source: Jick, McKersie, and Greenhalgh 1983: 187. Reprinted by permission of the Industrial Relations Research Association,© 1983.

Michael Schuster (1983:194) points out that the evidence strongly suggests that "cooperation cannot be imposed at the plant level by actors external to the immediate bargaining relationship." When programs are started nationally, a strong effort must be made to convince plant-level participants of the need for change.

Many experts also find that agreement on fundamental problems and ultimate goals is essential. So too is the presence of competent people knowledgeable about devising and implementing cooperative strategies. At the same time, participants must recognize that participative systems are inherently time consuming

Conclusions

We set out in this report to evaluate cooperative programs in light of where they have been, where they are in the mid-1980s, and where they may be going in the future. One conclusion is clear. Despite their somewhat uncertain past, enthusiasm for such projects persists. At the same time, however, there is a growing awareness, based on increasing experience with a variety of projects, of the inherent problems in creating programs that will be mutually satisfactory over a long period of time to the majority of those involved. Ultimately, the question comes down to whether these programs can be sustained. To meet the test, labor-management cooperation must be deemed to be a valuable addition to the industrial scene by employees and representatives of both unions and management—in good times and bad.

Experience over the past ten years shows that where cooperative programs have been instituted in organized firms, with or without union participation, the relationship between labor and management—and between collective bargaining and cooperative problem solving—has not always been totally successful. A 1984 report of a conference conducted by the U.S. Department of Labor (DOL), attended by twenty-five representatives of labor, management, and academia, illustrates the point.

Participants were presented with a relatively optimistic position paper in which it was argued that "with time and experience, relationships, trust, and skills will build between the parties so that issues over inherent differences between QWL and CB [collective bargaining] will lose much of their force" and that "although the CB process and QWL are not interchangeable, the two will interact and influence each other in ways that benefit both" (U.S. DOL 1984:3-4).

The position paper recognized the inherent differences between the two approaches, one adversarial and relying on bargaining or power for agreement, and the other cooperative, based on reaching consensus through trust and information sharing. The position taken was that the QWL approach could produce more optimal results than bargaining alone, if certain safeguards were maintained.

Discussions among participants at the conference, on the other hand, reflected "strong traditional concerns, many of which supported a very clear separation of CB and QWL" (U.S. DOL 1984:5). Labor representatives saw a substantial danger in giving up any legally binding collective bargaining for voluntary agreements that could be unilaterally abrogated. They were suspicious that QWL could be used to circumvent a union through corporate paternalism and were wary of cooperating in one plant while work was moved to nonorganized facilities.

Participants were willing to concede that cooperative programs could succeed where a mature bargaining relationship exists, where organized labor is accepted as a legitimate and permanent partner, and where there is a greater sharing of information. They concluded, however, that "because individual companies and unions are at different stages in their labor relations development...the relationship between QWL and collective bargaining should reflect the needs of each situation, and should not be rushed or moved along at any predetermined speed" (U.S. DOL 1984:6).

The attitudes of these representatives of labor, management, and academia probably represent those of a large number of practitioners in the field. These attitudes suggest that while union and management leaders may be willing to experiment with cooperative programs, the acceptance and success of such programs will vary from organization to organization, based upon the perspectives of the parties, the stability of their employment relationship, and the status of their collective bargaining.

Although there are some very visible examples of cooperative programs in nonunionized organizations, for the most part they operate in the manufacturing sector, which tends to be organized. As noted earlier, James T. Mills, the president of the Conference Board, suggests that there is currently a reappraisal of the way U.S. work forces are managed and that traditional assumptions about work and workers are being questioned. But this does not mean that cooperative work schemes, with an emphasis on worker control and decision making, have become the norm (Gorlin and Schein 1984: v).

In the nonunionized sector, the question of shared decision making, between employees and supervisors, becomes important, because managers often are faced with the prospect of joint decision making for the first time. By any standard, worker participation is still relatively limited in the United States. (Worker autonomy is even more limited.) Where participation does exist, it usually operates on a department or unit basis, functioning within well-defined limits.

Resistance to cooperative programs is due in part to the firmly held belief in American business of "management rights" and to the attitudes of certain managers who distrust the motives of those who champion shared decision making, who are fearful of change and the loss of status and power, and who question the costs of cooperative programs in relation to what they consider to be uncertain benefits. At the same time, however, there have been companies that have been willing to adopt a more venturesome approach. As pointed out in the U.S. Department of Labor report:

> The issue here is that you tend to get what you aim for. If your purpose in engaging in QWL is narrow—to buy a little "labor peace," to get some improvements in productivity and quality—you will aim at getting that, and you might get what you want, enough of it to feel satisfied, anyway. And, it might—if you do it "right"—sustain itself for what seems an indeterminate time. Moreover, you might be able to do this without getting into those hairy questions of "shared decision making."
>
> But if you want an organization whose people are fully engaged, "turned-on," if you will, and which, as a result, seeks excellence, continuous improvement, and adaptive efficiency to a changing world—then you must come to a decision to pursue the broadest kinds of QWL transformations carefully and pragmatically. Here, "shared decision-making" in various carefully worked-out ways is assumed to be a part of what you want (U.S. DOL 1984:7).

In many ways, the mid-1980s continue to be a period of crisis. Although inflation is stabilized and the nation is no longer in the throes of a recession, management is still at considerable risk, faced with increased foreign competition and major problems in productivity. At the same time, organized labor is confronted with a significant decline in membership and is concerned about the plummeting number of jobs available in manufacturing. In the early 1950s, for example, union membership constituted 33 percent of the American work force. A decade ago, the figure had dropped to 29 percent, and in 1985, the unions' share was just 19 percent. Unions now are winning 45 percent of their representation elections in comparison to 75 percent in the mid-50s (Greenhouse 1985:6F).

The fact that crisis spawns an interest in cooperation bodes well for the continued experimentation with these programs. It remains to be seen whether unions are seeking—and managements providing—such benefits as employee participation in decision making and increased quality of life on the job because (a) they are finding it difficult to give employees major improvements in basic wages and other standard conditions of employment, (b) they are responding to the needs of a new, younger work force that sees these benefits as an essential part of their work life, or (c) they basically believe in the value of joint decision making. There is no doubt, however, that these forces are creating dramatic new changes in the workplace.

One striking example is that of the agreement between the UAW and the General Motors Corporation for the manufacture of the company's new Saturn car. John Holusha in the *New York Times* described the agreement as calling for "a level of cooperation between management and labor that has few precedents in American heavy industry" (1985:6). The project was developed to offset the cost and quality advantages enjoyed by Japanese over American companies in the production of small cars. An emphasis is placed on consensus in decision making and the involvement of workers on committees operating on the shop floor as well as at all other levels of management. The agreement also calls for increased job security, blocking the layoff of at least 80 percent of the workers involved, "barring unforeseen or catastrophic events" (which will be determined by a Strategic Advisory Committee composed of union and management representatives).

Topics of decision making are broad, ranging from labor-management issues to such matters as selecting suppliers of parts and equipment. As of this writing, however, the limits of decision-making responsibility remain unclear. While workers have representation on committees that administer the Saturn plant and those that develop long-range strategy, they appear to have only advisory powers, with management making the final decisions. At other levels of the organization, according to the agreement, "Any of the parties may block a potential decision. However, the party blocking the decision must search for alternatives. In the event an alternative solution is not found, the blocking party must re-evaluate the position in the context of the philosophy and mission." Holusha concludes that "while the union could dissent and delay, it could probably not stop a determined management without jeopardizing the good will both sides agree is essential to the success of Saturn" (1985:6).

In the introduction to this report, we noted that for labor-management committees and QWL projects to play, and be perceived as playing, a central role in relations between employers and employees, cooperative projects would have to be embraced by the unionized sector of the economy and would have to serve as the basis for a new working relationship in the nonunionized sector. That has not taken place. But what has occurred is an increased willingness to consider and implement programs that may well form the basis for a new relationship among these key groups. What we have seen during the past ten years is an industrial experiment of significant proportions. What occurs during the next ten years may well determine whether these programs are viable or whether they are little more than a periodic passing fancy.

REFERENCES

Abel, I. W.
1974 *Employment Security and Plant Productivity Committees: Ten Coordinating Steel Companies.* Washington, D.C.: National Commission on Productivity and Work Quality.

Ahern, Robert W.
1983 "Discussion." In *Proceedings of the Thirty-fifth Annual Meeting, Industrial Relations Research Association,* edited by Barbara D. Dennis, pp. 201-6. Madison, Wisc.: IRRA.

Anderson, John C., and Peter Feuille
1981 "The Existence and Effectiveness of Labor-Management Committees" (a paper presented at the Thirty-fourth Annual Meeting of the Industrial Relations Research Association, December 20-30, 1981, Washington, D. C.).

Birbaum, Alan
1982 "Union Views on Quality of Work Life" (a paper prepared for the Industrial Union Department of the AFL-CIO, Fall).

Bluestone, Irving
1974 "Decision Making by Workers." *Personnel Administrator* 19 (July-August): 26-30.

1980 "How Quality-of-Worklife Projects Work for the United Auto Workers." *Monthly Labor Review* 103 (July): 39-41.

Business Week
1971 "Labor Chills Talk about Productivity." No. 2189 (August 14): 29-30.

1972 "The Unions Begin to Bend on Work Rules." No. 2263 (September 9): 100-108.

Camens, Sam
1982 Statement of Sam Camens, Assistant to the President, United Steelworkers of America, on Labor-Management Participation Teams in the Basic Steel Industry Before the Subcommittee on Oversight and Investigation, U.S. House of Representatives (April 23).

Canada, Department of Labour
1966 *Today's Need for Joint Consultation.* Ottawa: R. Duhamel.

CWEP/QWL&P
1981 *CWEP/QWL&P Subcommittee.* A brochure published by the State of New York, September 24.

Daily Labor Report (BNA)
1983 "Federal Aid to Labor-Management Panels Justified by Results, Participants Say." No. 108 (June 3): A-1—A-2 and D-1—D-2.

Davey Harold W.
1968 "Union-Management Cooperation Revisited." *Business Prospectives* 14 (Winter): 4-10.

Derber, Milton
1970a *The American Idea of Industrial Democracy, 1865-1965.* Urbana: University of Illinois Press.

1970b "Crosscurrents in Workers Participation." *Industrial Relations* 9 (February): 123-36.

de Schweinitz, Dorothea
1949 *Labor and Management in a Common Enterprise.* Cambridge, Mass.: Harvard University Press.

Douty, H. M.
1974 "Labor-Management Productivity Committees in American Industry." Unpublished report prepared for the National Commission on Productivity and Work Quality.

Dubin, Robert
1949 "Labor-Management Co-operation and Productivity." *Industrial and Labor Relations Review* 2 (January): 195-209.

Ewing, David W.
1971 "Who Wants Corporate Democracy?" *Harvard Business Review* 49 (September-October): 12-28, 146-48.

Fuller, Stephen H.
1980 "How Quality-of-Worklife Projects Work for General Motors." *Monthly Labor Review* (July): 37-39.

Gompers, Samuel
1920 *Labor and the Employer.* New York: E. P. Dutton.

Gold, Charlotte
1976 *Employer-Employee Committees and Worker Participation,* Key

Issues No. 20. Ithaca: New York State School of Industrial and Labor Relations, Cornell University.

Goldoff, Anna
1978 "The Perceptions of Participants in a Joint Productivity Program." *Monthly Labor Review* (July): 33-34.

Gorlin, Harriet, and Lawrence Schein
1984 *Innovations in Managing Human Resources,* Report No. 849. New York: The Conference Board.

Greenberg, Leon
1973 *A Practical Guide to Productivity Measurement.* Washington, D.C.: Bureau of National Affairs.

Greenhouse, Steven
1985 "Reshaping Labor to Woo the Young." *New York Times*, September 1 (Sec. 3): 1 and 6.

Hanlon, Martin D.
1981 Unions and the QWL Movement." *QWL Review* 1 (Fall): 8-13.

Hanlon, Martin D., and John C. Williams
1982 "In Jamestown: Labor-Management Committee at Work." *QWL Review* 1 (Summer): 2-8.

Hartnett, Thomas F.
1982 "QWL's Impact on CSEA Agreement."*QWL Review* 1(Summer): 12-14.

Hoerr, John
1982 "A New Friend for Quality of Work Life." *Business Week* (September 27): 26.

Holusha, John
1985 "G.M. Contract Aims to Foster Union-Management Cooperation." *New York Times* July 28 (Sec. 4): 4 and 6.

Jenkins, David
1973 *Job Power: Blue and White Collar Democracy.* Garden City, N.Y.: Doubleday.

Jick, Todd D., Robert McKersie , and Leonard Greenhalgh
1983 "A Process Analysis of Labor-Management Committee Problem-Solving." In *Proceedings of the Thirty-fifth Annual Meeting, Industrial Relations Research Association,* edited by Barbara D. Dennis, pp. 182-88. Madison, Wisc.: IRRA.

Lazes, Peter, and Tony Costanza
1984 "Xerox Cuts Costs without Layoffs through Union-Management Collaboration." *Labor-Management Cooperation Brief* (July).

Leone, Richard D.
1983 "Area-Wide Labor-Management Committees: Where Do We Go from Here?" In *Proceedings of the Thirty-fifth Annual Meeting, Industrial Relations Research Association*, edited by Barbara D. Dennis, pp. 173-81. Madison, Wisc.: IRRA.

Maccoby, Michael
1984 "Helping Labor and Management Set Up a Quality-of-Worklife Program." *Monthly Labor Review* (March): 28-32.

Michaels, Marguerite
1984 "Can Labor Unions Survive?" *Parade Magazine* (September 2): 14-15.

Metzger, Bert
1974 "Profit Sharing USA." *Industrial Participation*, No. 554 (Spring): 17-25.

National Commission on Productivity and Work Quality (NCPWQ)
1973 *Ten Questions and Answers on Productivity.* Washington, D.C.: GPO.

Nation's Business
1973 "Speaking Out for Better Output." Vol. 61 (November): 62-65.

PEWS
n.d. *Programs for Employment and Workplace Systems.* A brochure published by the Extension Division, New York State School of Industrial and Labor Relations, Cornell University.

QWL Review
1981 "An Interview with Irving Bluestone." Vol 1 (Fall): 13-18.

1983 "Private Sector Report: Ford Employee Involvement at Green Island, N.Y." Vol. 3 (September): 16-18.

Raskin, A. H.
1975 "Labor: Public Aggression, Private Cooperation." *New York Times*, August 31 (Sec.3): 1 and 5.

Roback, Leo
1970 "Industrial Democracy: Definitions, Questions and Problems." In *Industrial Democracy and Canadian Labour*, pp. 4-21. Toronto:

Ontario Woodsworth Memorial Foundation and Praxis Research Institute for Social Change.

Robbins, John R.
1972 "Workers' Participation and Industrial Democracy: Variations on a Theme." *Journal of Industrial Relations* 14 (December): 427-38.

Schraeger, Barbara
1983 "QWL in San Francisco." *QWL Review* 1 (September): 13.

Schuster, Michael
1983 "Problems and Opportunities in Implementing Cooperative Union-Management Programs." In *Proceedings of the Thirty-fifth Annual Meeting, Industrial Relations Research Association*, edited by Barbara D. Dennis, pp. 189-97. Madison, Wisc.: IRRA.

Serrin, William
1984 "Giving Workers a Voice of Their Own." *New York Times Magazine* (December 2): 126-32, 136-37.

Slichter, Sumner H.
1941 *Union Policies and Industrial Management.* Washington, D.C.: Brookings Institution.

Sockell, Donna
1984 "The Legality of Employee-Participation Programs in Unionized Firms." *Industrial and Labor Relations Review* 37 (July): 541-56.

Stepina, Lee P.
1982 "No Free Lunch: Labor-Management Productivity Committees." *National Public Employment Reporter* 5 (November): 5-11.

Strauss, George, and Eliezer Rosenstein
1971 "Workers Participation: A Critical View." *Industrial Relations* 9 (February): 197-214.

Sturmthal, Adolf
1968 *Workers' Participation in Management: A Review of the United States Experience.* Country Studies Series. Bulletin 6. Geneva: International Institute for Labour Studies.

Thrasher, Bruce
1973 "Joint Labor-Management Approach to Productivity—The Steel Industry." In *Proceedings of the Conference on Productivity: Its Impact on Collective Bargaining and Employee Relations*, pp. 9-20. Nashville: University of Tennessee, Institute for Public Service.

U.S. Department of Labor
1984 *A Conference on Quality of Work Life: Issues Affecting the State-of-the-Art*. Washington, D.C.: U.S. Department of Labor, Office of Labor-Management Relations Services.

U.S. News and World Report
1973 "When Workers and Bosses Join to Boost Efficiency." Vol. 74 (April 16): 121-22.

Vroom, Victor H.
1964 *Work and Motivation*. New York: Wiley.

Watts, Glenn
1983 "QWL: CWA's Position." *QWL Review* 1 (March): 12.

ACKNOWLEDGMENTS

The author wishes to express her appreciation for their helpful critiques and suggestions to Bernard Flaherty, Central District Director of Extension, and Donald D. Kane, Director of Programs for Employment and Workplace Systems, at the New York State School of Industrial and Labor Relations, Cornell University; and to James B. Northrop, Director of Workforce Planning, in the New York Governor's Office of Employee Relations. She thanks again Professor Felician F. Foltman and Rodney E. Dennis who directed a two-day conference in January 1975 for the New York State School of Industrial and Labor Relations in cooperation with the National Commission on Productivity and Work Quality—a conference that first focused her attention on labor-management committees. She also wishes to express appreciation to the staff of the ILR press and specifically to Jozetta H. Srb, editor of the *Key Issues* series, whose advice and assistance in the preparation of this publication were especially helpful.

Charlotte Gold
March 1986